PLANNING PERMISSION
EXPERTISE FOR
BUILDINGS AND EXTENSIONS

Architect Knowhow Publishing

PLANNING PERMISSION EXPERTISE FOR BUILDINGS AND EXTENSIONS

A Step-by-Step Guide by a Chartered Architect

Dr. **WILLIAM J. HOGAN-O'NEILL** RIBA. ARB.

Book One - How to get Started
Pre-Planning

Architect®
Knowhow.

First Published in 2022 by
Architect Knowhow Publishing
85 Great Portland Street First Floor London W1W 7LT

dr.william@architectknowhow.com
www.architectknowhow.com

British Library Cataloguing-Publication-Data
A catalogue record for this book is available from the British Library

ISBN   978 1 915308 00 9

Dedication
To Gemma and Harriet

The Perfect Checklist for Getting Organised and Keeping Control of Your Project!

www.architectknowhow.com

Get Yourself Organised with these 10 Actions:

Getting Organised

Gather Site and Planning Information

Verify Status of the Site / Property

Examine Your Planning Options

Carry Out Detail Checks

Commence Concept Design Development

Prepare for Your Pre-Application

Prepare Your Planning Drawings & Documents

Decision to proceed with Planning Submission

Planning Period Begins

Contents

Contents

Contents

Your Objective

I know from experience when people think about new buildings, renovations, and building extensions, one of the first thoughts that comes to mind will inevitably surround winning that planning permission. Achieving that elusive planning permission is the big prize, and you do not have to allow your site or property to become a total gamble when it comes to realising a planning permission. Achieving your planning permission can be more realistic when you have a better understanding of what is involved, what the process is, and what you need to know.

I feel your pain

If there is one factor alone that creates havoc and turmoil for consultants, agents, and property owners alike, it will be all the planning challenges each site and its location will attract. For agents, consultants and property owners, these planning issues, problems, headaches, and heartaches are well known. Problematic matters are not always the same because every site situation and location will generate their own unique planning situations and circumstances.

The pain connected with all of this planning calamity begins with not knowing what to expect at the start and not being in control of the process as you must. As you try to find your way through this malaise of planning debacles there is no knowing sometimes what type of objections or special conditions you will have to deal with.

Even with all the time, costs, and effort you invest in making a planning application there is still no certainty of achieving your planning permission as you might reasonably expect. This is primarily because the UK planning system is a discretionary regime. Discretionary means exactly that and it will be your local planning authority who will decided. Moreover, planning decisions are not necessarily decided by clearly established rules because there are non. There are of course planning policies Neighbourhood Plans and some design guides which, can be interpreted in any number of ways, as indeed they often are. Planning decisions for your site or land are often dictated by your local planning authority's preferences, their political masters and sometimes influenced by objectors who makes a career of promoting 'no' as the preferred option.

A solution does exist

The solution to all of this calamity is firstly, knowing there is a process to all of this planning regime. The pre-planning process is what takes place before you make your final planning submission, and therefore, your upfront preparation is a vital element in order to achieve planning success.

This pre-planning preparation is what is described and discussed in this book.

It is an introduction to the whole pre-planning process and will provide you with a comprehensive overview of what is expected when it comes to preparing and presenting a viable design solution to your local planning authority.

You will obtain an excellent insight into the process and procedures in a very simple easy to read text. It will provide you with answers to many of the initial questions you would like to ask an architect once you start thinking about your property and dealing with planning matters. You will achieve a greater understanding of what each site and its location means in terms of satisfying your local planning authority. You will know what preparation is required in order to make a planning submission which has integrity where the architectural design solution you put forward meets the criteria expected by your local planning authority.

What you will learn

Whilst it is not necessary for you to become a planning expert per se, you will be introduced to some essential elements in how to get yourself organised and the rudiments that are vital for your planning submission to achieve success.

This means recognising aspects like the attributes your site or property has to offer as well as constraints which have the opposite effect - your site location and what its context and character means - its relationship to adjoining properties and what that might mean also and more besides. Explaining these elements to your local planning authority in your planning submission with highlighting how your design proposal is a 'good fit' can have a profound influence on the viability of your project thereby justifying a planning permission as a likely outcome.

By reading this book you will discover the benefits of recognising what your local planning authority normally expects as a well considered planning submission. There is much more to preparing a planning submission than a set of basic drawings with scant information.

You will be introduced to some fundamental principles and essential information your local planning authority will prefer which means going beyond the minimum for a planning submission. By explaining your development site and why your architectural design solution is appropriate for your site and its location in a meaningful way, you will provide the planners the means to grant you your planning permission as a natural outcome.

In order for you to know how to reduce your planning risk and increase your scope for planning permission success it is necessary to refer to an information source that will guide your through this process and explain the various elements surrounding the preparation of a planning submission in a logical and methodical way.

I'm an architect - this is what I do

As a chartered architect I have prepared numerous types of planning applications over my thirty-seven years in professional practice. I can vouch for the fact that being armed with a well researched, well considered and well prepared planning submission offers the best opportunity of achieving that elusive planning permission.

In this book and other books in my pre-planning series, I am sharing with you the knowledge, experience, and expertise that I have acquired as an architect in practice so as to help you achieve the best results possible for your development site.

I want you to enjoy this easy to read book as the first book in the pre-planning series. It will take you though most of what you need to know first, and then, what you should be thinking about for your planning permission. It will set the ground for you to delve into more detailed information and knowhow in the following books.

You are invited to join our facebook group and to visit our website which provides more Architect Knowhow.

dr.william@architectknowhow.com

Chapter One

Where to Begin

Before the life of a building, a group of buildings, or any building complex can begin, there is a conception of sorts brought about by an individual property owner, real estate developer, central or local government body, or private or public body seeking to achieve an objective. It begins there: someone with an idea and belief seeking to achieve betterment for mankind and an enrichment of lives, as well as to make a profit.

As humans occupying this planet, we have evolved from needing caves to creating structures and primitive huts as shelter to eventually building a plethora of structures ranging from apartment tower blocks and houses and extensions to medical centres, educational establishments, community buildings, and recreation

An early stone structure Llun y gromlech Wales. (Image by Marthuws)

facilities. We continue to require buildings and structures of various shapes and sizes dictated to a large degree by our location, climate, and cultural preferences, from which our built environments are shaped accordingly.

Most organised societies recognise the necessity to control the way in which our buildings, structures, and spaces are created and developed, an endeavour in which planning control is deemed a natural part of the process.

Whilst planning rules are intended to serve the best interests of our communities, there is inevitably a measure of contention when it comes to obtaining a planning permission. In this regard, the UK planning process is often seen as a weapon employed by those in power or those seeking to prevent certain developments from taking place as opposed to being a means to facilitate new community development and new architecture as an evolving culture and society.

That elusive planning permission will always remain the prize, as the journey of achieving it can be arduous. However, having a simple appreciation for what is involved and adopting the procedures necessary for preparing a well-considered planning submission is the key factor for planning success.

In terms of humankind occupying this planet Earth, it is only relatively recently that planning rules and regulations became popular within certain fraternities and a reluctant acceptance for the rest, perhaps. Now that humans are venturing off to

Exploring environments beyond Earth. (Courtesy of NASA)

environments beyond the boundaries of this planet, it begs the question: At what point will planners and urban designers begin to dictate planning legislation for our new worlds, or will it be left to the space engineers?

Necessary Information

Back on earth however, the focus here is to flush out the usual problems and difficulties that the planning system always seems to present. To highlight many of those usual tricky bits and fiddly situations that can arise before you actually make your planning submission to your local planning authority. The important factor associated with any planning submission is that you are seeking to ensure a well-considered submission is prepared in the first instance which will ultimately adhere with the goals and aspirations set by your local planning authority. Simultaneously, you must ensure that the resulting building or development will also be right for you or your client.

Whether you are an individual land or property owner with an enthusiasm for self-management, a budding real estate or project manager, or an architectural, surveying, or other construction student seeking to understand and know more about this unpredictable world of planning, this pre-planning book series will provide you with some vital insights and knowhow. It will grant you a starting point and the skills to get yourself organised from the beginning of the process.

This four-part book series will provide you with an experienced, qualified archi-

tect's insight into identifying and dealing with those potential pitfalls as well as those fiddly situations usually associated with trying to get a building project off the ground. It will assist you in organising your thinking and thereby your approach when assessing your property and the land upon which it is located, helping you to evaluate its potential when preparing a planning submission. Before any submission is made to your local planning authority, therefore, the secret is to focus fully on the preparation of the pre-planning process, which is the most crucial element of the planning process.

Just so you know, having your property located in a specific location within a particular lane, a road or street - whether it is within a country, urban, or city environment - is not an issue for your local planning authority. Irrespective of whether your property relates to a residential or nonresidential development, they will review the merits of your proposal for that location as they see it at the time of your planning submission and decide accordingly.

It is, however, a major factor for you, as it is you who must demonstrate how appropriateness is satisfied, how suitability will be met, and how enhancement and benefit will be derived from your completed building/development. It is worth bearing in mind that through your planning submission, you are seeking to establish and introduce a new physical presence by way of a new building, a new addition or renovation, or perhaps you are seeking a change of use for your existing property. Consequently, it will be incumbent upon you to explain how your development proposal represents an appropriate design solution for your specific site and location in order to demonstrate a planning permission is well justified.

The whole business of acquiring a planning permission revolves around a process within which there are a variety of different parts and elements. The process necessary for you to obtain the desired planning permission will generally depend on the nature and extent of your project for your site, whether it is a simple domestic

Development site for new housing within an existing suburban built environment. (Drawing by Architect Knowhow)

extension or something more complex like a housing development, a business premises, or a commercial development. In essence, then, it is incumbent upon the property owner and/or their agent to recognise the actual application site for what it is, what it represents, and to understand its context within its built environment as well as the goals and aspirations of the local authority.

Consequently, to demonstrate and justify why your planning proposal should be granted a planning permission will necessitate more than a set of drawings and simply completing an application form. Similarly, there is clearly much more to a planning submission than merely assessing the profit margin on completion of the works on site; that does not require much apart from the ability to operate a calculator. Planning authorities throughout the UK are familiar with submissions of this calibre and frankly they often fail to impress the planning case officers dealing with your planning submission.

To provide yourself or your client with every possible opportunity for success, a commitment to preparing your planning submission properly is the key factor; your research and investigations are crucial. In other words, there is a heap of information that you need to know about your development site. Decisions must be made about how best to incorporate local planning policies into your final design solution for the site, all of which is what really matters to your local planning authority. A major part of the planning process, then, is your pre-planning stage. The pre-planning stage is where all your research and preparation work is done upfront and some concept ideas are explored—all before you consider making a planning submission.

Former motor showroom and workshops site offering a new development opportunity. (Image by Author)

Some Quick Advice

I often have people approach me - sometimes during and sometimes outside of business hours - asking for information or what my thinking might be in relation to a particular parcel of land or a building which has come to the market. In most cases, these off-the-cuff enquirers are well-intentioned requests from clients I may have collaborated with on projects in the past.

In reality, though, it is almost impossible to provide an off-the-cuff response that has any meaning without undertaking some level of enquiry or investigation. This will necessitate some simple assessment and analysis of the land or building in question. In almost every case, the topic will relate to planning with the objective of adding value - usually monetary value, as far as the client is concerned.

For many enquiries that come to me where the client needs to investigate to the next level, it would mean engaging my practice to undertake that work for them, an effort for which a fee would

become due. Most people who are blessed with a building opportunity are not lacking the comprehension necessary to tackle the initial site research and investigations themselves, especially when provided with access to the appropriate information and a methodology for managing that process.

Similarly, most agents or architectural students that I have come across, as well as students who have joined my own practice, have a reasonable grasp on what might be involved from their lectures, perhaps, but were not necessarily acquainted with the specifics or exposed to the cut and thrust of leading the process for getting a project underway. That is the heart of where to start and how to begin.

To assist you in approaching your project in an organised and methodical manner, I have coordinated the information you need to familiarise yourself with into four distinct entities.

To apply some context for you and help identify where you may be at this point in the process, let us assume you are starting at the beginning, which is clearly a good place to start. However, perhaps in your case you have already kicked off your project and could already be at any point in preparing your planning application. For instance, irrespective of what stage you are at, you may have already acquired your site; maybe you are about to acquire your site or a building which also has a parcel of land that could be developed. Perhaps you are managing your project, either on your own behalf or that of a client, and some further mentoring in the art and skills connected with managing the planning submission process is what you are looking for right now. With all of that in mind, you are nonetheless on a fact-finding mission as to what is involved in the overall process for achieving a planning permission, which is the particular focus of this book series.

It is not my intention here to cover every aspect associated with a building project;

that would be impossible, especially in any degree of detail that would be useful. I mainly want to focus on emphasising what should be considered for the 'up-front' elements of making your planning submission, as this is where the most important decisions have to be made.

Therefore, the emphasis is on the preparation, and my wish for you is to know that the preparation of a comprehensive and competent planning submission which will have meaning is always based on the information and intelligence resulting from your research and investigations. I believe this to be the correct approach, as opposed to cramming in superficial information on a multitude of topics covering the whole of a construction project which are not really relevant when it comes to achieving planning permissions. Achieving

---

Tel: 020 8921 5222

ROYAL *borough of* GREENWICH

Mr Delle
DWD
  New Bridge Street
London
EC4V 6AB

Directorate of Regeneration, Enterprise & Skills
The Woolwich Centre, 5th Floor
35 Wellington Street
London, SE18 6HQ

21/2604/NM

18 August 2021
DECISION NOTICE (NON MATERIAL AMENDMENT REFUSED)

Dear Mr Deller,

Town & Country Planning Act 1990 (As Amended)
Town & Country Planning (Development Management Procedure)(England) Order 2015

Site: WESTHORNE AVENUE, ELTHAM, LONDON, SE9 5LT
Applicant:
Proposal: An application submitted under Section 96a of the Town & Country Planning Act 1990 for a non material amendment in connection with

Local Planning Authority informing the applicant the changes being sought to an existing planning permission are significant and will necessitate a fresh planning application

the planning permission is the most vital part of the enterprise, as without your planning permission in place, there is no project. Therefore, I seek only to assist you with the pre-planning process, as that is where your planning submission begins.

To help you achieve this objective, therefore, I have compiled this pre-planning information into four books where each book will cover specific aspects of the pre-planning process in an organised, methodical, and sequential manner, taking you through each step of the process as they tend to occur. The intention is to make the information available to you as you progress through the preparation process and to make it more digestible and meaningful as well as present the information in manageable chunks.

Planning Permission

Burnley
.gov.uk

M⸱ M⸱⸱⸱⸱ W⸱att
2   ce Park   S⸱⸱⸱⸱⸱⸱ A⸱⸱⸱nue
L⸱   Burr
P   BB1⸱ ⸱⸱ ⸱⸱⸱
P⸱⸱⸱ ⸱⸱⸱

Part 1   Particulars of Application: FUL/2020/   received 12th August 2020

Proposal: Erection of single dwelling and garage with associated infrastructure.

Location: Southern Avenue Burnley Lancashire

Part 2 Particulars of Decision:

The Council gives notice under the Town and Country Planning Act 1990 (as amended) that Planning Permission has been Granted for the carrying out of the development in accordance with the application and plans submitted, referred to in Part 1 above, and subject to the following conditions and reasons:

Some typical Decision Notices issued by local planning authorities

DELEGATED REPORT

Application Number: ₁₀/₀₂../FUL

Decision Due by: 11th October 201

Proposal: Formation of 1No. dormer window to west roofslope, 1No. dormer window and insertion of 2No. rooflights to north roofslope and insertion of 1No. window to east elevation in association with loft conversion.

Site Address: Frenchay Road Oxford OX2 6TF

Ward: St Margarets Ward

Agent: Mr Ro.... .... | **Applicant:** Mr & Mrs ....

Recommendation:

APPLICATION BE REFUSED

For the Following Reasons:-

1   Due to its flat roof form design and projection beyond the existing roof slope, the proposed dormers would interrupt the regular rhythm of the buildings and roof lines. It would create an incongruous roof form and overly bulky addition that would form an unacceptable visual relationship with the existing host building, and would fail to enhance or preserve the character of the main roof and the façade of the host building. As such the proposal would fail to comply with policies CP1, CP8, and CP10 of Oxford Local Plan, CS18 of the Core Strategy and HP9 of Sites and Housing Plan.

Standard flat roof approach to dormer window being refused by Local Planning Authority because it is not visually compatible with the existing built form.

An Overview of This Pre-Planning Book Series

Book One - How to Get Started

This book will introduce you to what usually has to be investigated, examined, and explored as a natural part of obtaining a planning permission. It will indicate what information you will need to know and explain why researching and investigating your site or property is vital when it comes to making decisions based on fact rather than a hope and a prayer.

Through this book, I have aimed to provide you with a comprehensive overview of what it means to prepare for and make a suitable planning submission. Whether you intend to manage the pre-planning process yourself or appoint a person to act for you, you will be far better equipped to interact and contribute to the pre-planning process after reading this book.

Whilst Book One will enlighten you about much of what needs to be considered up front, it will also introduce you to a mindset and thinking process when considering a development for your site or property. It prepares the groundwork for you to consider your property in relation to its built environment, context, and character and highlights how your local planning authority will approach your planning submission.

You will be introduced to some important key insights about what might be involved for your project by assessing and analysing

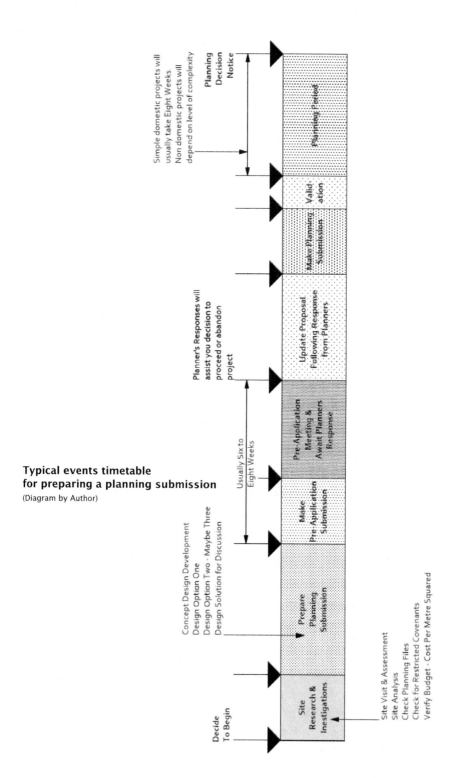

**Typical events timetable
for preparing a planning submission**
(Diagram by Author)

Decide
To Begin

Site
Research &
Inestigations

Site Visit & Assessment
Site Analysis
Check Planning Files
Check for Restricted Covenants
Verify Budget - Cost Per Metre Squared

Prepare
Planning
Submission

Concept Design Development
Design Option One
Design Option Two - Maybe Three
Design Solution for Discussion

Make
Pre-Application
Submission

Usually Six to
Eight Weeks

Pre-Application
Meeting &
Await Planners
Response

Planner's Responses will
assist you decision to
proceed or abandon
project

Update Proposal
Following Response
from Planners

Make Planning
Submission

Valid-
ation

Planning
Decision
Notice

Planning Period

Simple domestic projects will
usually take Eight Weeks
Non domestic projects will
depend on level of complexity

your research and findings. You will be able to grasp a simple, commonsense understanding of the surrounding context for your property's location, its built environment, and what this might mean for your project.

How to Get Started does exactly that; it gets you thinking about what you should be considering and clarifies what this preplanning process represents and why applying some serious thought to the enterprise is necessary for success.

Research and Investigation

By the time you have examined and explored the information and directions within How to Get Started, you will have a better grasp and understanding of the overall process generally and what might apply more specifically to your particular project. It will also be the right time for you to move on and consider your project in more detail, to give some serious thought to what options might be available for your project depending on its nature, size, and location.

Having the benefit of a tried and tested structure for you to follow and work towards when researching and investigating your site or property to refine it to the next level is the primary objective for preparing your planning submission. Book Two - Research and Investigation book will assist you in assessing and evaluating your research results and findings in relation to (a) your building site where your land /site does not have an existing property on it or (b) the nature and extent of your land/site which does have an existing

building and where you intended to extend it or demolish and rebuild.

Having absorbed and evaluated your research information in conjunction with assessing your site or property, this insight will allow you to decide if actually proceeding any further with preparing a planning submission for a particular site or property is the correct option for you. *Research and Investigation* will give you the wherewithal to gather sufficient knowhow to arrive at a stage in the pre-planning process to decide whether your project has a reasonable chance of being approved. This will tell you also whether continuing with the particular site or property that you are considering is the correct option for you or whether an alternative site or property might be a better proposition. In order words, you might find it is time to pull out and walk away, because there are always alternative real estate opportunities that are less contentious for what you seek to achieve.

Undertaking the value this research and investigation phase represents and concluding on the validity of the project early on will give you the first indication as to whether your project for a specific site or property is the correct option for you. If it is, move on to Book Three, which will take you through the next crucial stage of your process. This third book has a total focus on possible attributes and constraints attached to your property and explains what they might mean when preparing your planning submission.

Attributes and Constraints

Attributes and constraints are usually connected with sites or property. In Book Three I refer to them as attributes and constraints rather than 'pros and cons' because they are more meaningful labels when it comes to describing their relationship to property/real estate development. This is a very important part of your site research, as these findings can have a profound impact on your process.

In the case of attributes, they can add immediate benefit and value to your project, both for the pre-planning stage and the subsequent construction stage. Reference is made to how existing attributes your site may possess can add value not only in a monetary sense but also in how they assist your design proposal in planning and architecture terms, thereby justifying your local planning authority to grant you permission to develop your property. Planning policy and architectural design will be the primary interest of the planning authority more so than any monetary gain, unlike the developer, of course, where turning a profit is the primary objective. Similarly, there may also be attributes that exist on the perimeter edges to your site or property which can also play a significant part in contributing further planning and architectural merit and enhancement to your proposal which you get for free. I will highlight some of these also so you will know how to use them.

Then there are constraints, which are always the 'bogeymen' in matters relating to planning. I highlight constraints in much greater detail and explain how these can have a negative impact on your project. Constraints can impose themselves during the pre-planning stages, during the construction stage, or both, but you should be aware of any potential constraints up front at the pre-planning stage before you even begin to spend money on the project.

I give a great deal of attention to constraints because I know from my experience in practice how these factors can influence the viability of a project for a client. Constraints attached to your site can have an influence on decisions made by your local planning authority too. They can also be a deciding factor for a client in assessing the viability of a project not only by their financial implications but in some cases the sheer hassle factor they always seem to attract. Their time-consuming nature can similarly bring into question whether the enterprise is really worthwhile.

Having an early indication as to the viability of your project in terms of achieving the planning permission you are seeking is a very good place to start, and having a grasp on any site constraints is part of that viability test. Consequently, by assessing and analysing your research findings as well as developing a simple, commonsense understanding of architectural context for your property's location, you will have acquired some fundamental ingredients which are key factors for creating a successful planning submission. You will be in a very good place to evaluate the impact of any constraints that may be attached to your site or property, and you will be better equipped to make meaningful decisions that direct you to what will be the best options for you. That is, do you abandon your development project for that site or property, or are there still good enough reason(s) for you to continue as originally intended?

Because there are so many matters to discuss relating to constraints and how they can impact your project in a very significant way, I have devoted a completed book to this specific topic. This was not my original intention, but as I researched my own project files and instances where constraints occur, I began to realise I could not sensibly deal with this topic within a chapter.

By the end of Book Three, you will have completed your research and evaluations to a point where you will have completed your site assessments/analyses sufficient for your purposes. You will be in an ideal position to decide if the final part of the application process is still worth pursuing for the site or property in question. Continuing to the final stage of the planning submission process will mean some money will have to be invested in having planning drawings prepared and submitting your planning application to your local planning authority. You will be better able to assess if this is the correct option for your site or property after assessing these constraints, and if you find it makes sense to move forward, taking on Book Four will feel like a natural progression.

The Planning Submission

Making a planning submission is the final stage of the pre-planning process. It deals with matters you should know about in order to make sure your UK planning submission is prepared correctly, such as making sure the required information is prepared, assembled, and submitted correctly. This will involve completing the planning application form, preparing the required drawing information, and completing other planning documents that are required, all of which will be dictated by the level of complexity linked with your development project.

Obtaining your planning permission is really the first approval that you will require. There are other approvals that are necessary in order for building work to commence on-site, though the precise nature and extent of such planning documents that may be required will be dictated by the nature and complexity of your project.

Author on site visit (Image by Practice colleague)

You should likewise be aware that whilst generally most domestic extensions and new builds are straight forward, even some simple domestic extensions can turn out to be complex for a variety of reasons, all of which revolve around the type of planning system that currently exists in the UK.

Book Four will also provide you with a strategy for appointing an architect or another consultant familiar with preparing your planning submission. It will also explain the remit of a fully qualified architect acting as your agent and differentiate this remit from a draughtsperson who can also act as your agent, both of whom have the ability to prepare planning drawings. I explain why some property owners believe (wrongly) that because they have drawings prepared and obtain a planning permission, the builder can start construction the following day.

Therefore, I also discuss what your local planning authority are more likely to be interested in and issues surrounding UK building control, also referred to as building regulations (US building permits). In parallel with this topic is the reference to working out likely building costs and affordability, and that is before you even make your planning submission, which itself has cost elements attached to it also.

In order to achieve a clear comprehension, a holistic account of what is involved for the whole of the planning preparation process, rest assured that you have now found the right information source to take you through the ins and outs of how to prepare your planning submission. As an information source, this book series provides an excellent all-round account of the pre-planning process. It explores the nature and extent of what actions are usually required to provide a better result for achieving your planning permission.

Ideally, I have properly underscored the immense importance of the pre-planning stage. It is all about the actions and decisions take place before you even submit your planning application or spend any money. An immediate piece of professional advice at the very initial stage is to not speak with builders yet, as you would be getting ahead of yourself. Any advice or information they may provide can be meaningless given some fundamental research and investigations must be carried out first (see Book Two: 'Avoid Duff Advice').

Deciding to Begin

The big takeaway from this heading is in the word 'deciding', and deciding to begin a project is a big commitment. Your research is truly vital when preparing a planning submission, as without it, your site knowledge and understanding of its surrounding built environment will be incomplete. Throughout the entire process of preparing your planning sub-mission, you will be introduced to and come across new information about your property at different stages. Much of the information you acquire will result from your own research and investigations, but you will also come across snippets of information from other sources along the way.

Your decision-making will be ongoing, and you will be required to make decisions

Learning how to make pre-planning Decisions. (Courtesy of Pixabay)

on certain aspects in order to move on to the next step in the process.

Deciding what is appropriate and relevant for your planning submission is not always simple or obvious. It is, however, based on the research information you gather together and how you assess those findings for relevance.

Some of these decisions might be difficult for you and that is understandable, particularly if you are not familiar with the business of preparing a planning submission or well acquainted with the nuances surrounding your planning strategy. There are two aspects that relate to your planning strategy. First, there is the information to discover about your site or property which will influence and shape your decision whether to achieve your actual planning application or not. You are focused on evaluating and assessing this information primarily to achieve the best planning result possible, and in some respects you may decide to adopt this approach above all other considerations. In other words,

perhaps your strategy is to achieve a planning permission solely to create added value and sell on irrespective of any expensive planning baggage that might attract as a result (see Chapter 4: 'Planning Conditions and What They Mean').

Second, decisions that you will make during the pre-planning stage will clearly influence the direction of the construction process. Ideally, you are seeking to achieve a result whereby the decisions you make for your planning submission will also be appropriate and sensible, as much as possible, for the construction process that will follow later. I do not mean that you need to be hypercareful and cautious or totally stressed out about your every thought and judgment you are likely to make in preparing your planning application. I am, however, stating that when you are preparing your planning submission, consider where options are available to make decisions during the pre-planning process that will facilitate the following construction process in a pragmatic and sensible way.

Self managing a building project is more than owning a hard hat. (Image by Karolina Grabowska)

Consequently, as part of the pre-planning process, the concept of making decisions is for the betterment of your property asset in the round, as it were, which should include the construction process. Making judgments and decisions on both planning and construction issues is always a better strategy to follow, especially if the objective is for you to undertake the management and execution of the construction element yourself or on behalf of your client.

During the pre-planning process, there will always be changes and adjustments, and therefore decisions must be made as a consequence. Sometimes even during the pre-planning process circumstances may change where new events will enter the mix both intentionally and unintentionally which will cause you to reevaluate the situation and your options. The status of your development project might be altered from what was originally intended, and what might be the best course of action for you as a result may have to change or be adjusted accordingly. The primary objective in any property development, however, is to create added value. In many cases this means the first consideration for all decisions taken will revolve around securing a planning permission of some description as a first priority.

I Can Do This

Self-managing, as with, say, the concept associated with 'self-build' or 'owner build', is not an uncommon option for many. It has connotations associated with saving money in order to make the project happen or it being a lifelong ambition, all of which are honourable and valid reasons for taking the role on.

Self designing a building or a home is not all unique. Even the most inspirational of design ideas are sometimes developed from existing design solutions. (Image by Daniel McCullough)

The self-builder's input into the construction process varies from doing the actual construction to appointing an architect and a building company. (Image by Author)

Achieving the completed building is often accomplished by the site or property owners themselves, employing expertise and knowledge already in their possession. You may have management ability, but you might also have some property or construction project management experience, in which case you are off to a good start. You may possess a particular skill or trade which you can employ in your project, and being familiar with the construction process, you will obviously have a better understanding of how the various construction processes progress from one stage to the next. You will also know what is likely and expected as a consequence.

However, many self-builders or owner builders do not possess every skill and trade expertise and in many cases they have no practical skills at all, thereby necessitating employing others who do. For instance, you may need to employ a qualified electrician to ensure the electrical installation is completed correctly and in compliance with the current regulations for the construction. You may also need to employ a roofer who is skilled and experienced in that trade and an expert in ensuring the roof to your new building will be weather-tight. Indeed, where you have no trade skills, you clearly have to employ the entire set of tradespersons and skills to complete the building for you, which naturally will form part of your overall project costs.

As you may be intending to manage your project yourself with or without any previous experience or as a person acting for your client as the agent, your primary function is precisely that: to manage. The concept of management, then, will apply whether you intended to engage in the pre-planning process first and the construction process subsequently, both of which require different skill sets, specialist knowledge, and expertise.

At this point in time, though, you are seeking only to achieve your planning permission or whatever certificate or approval (see Book Two: 'Planning and Permitted Development') is required for the jurisdiction your land or property is located within. You are seeking to secure the necessary approvals which will allow you to build your new building or extension on land you own. Perhaps you are seeking to extend or undertake major renovations to an existing building, or perhaps you are seeking to obtain a change of use, all of which will form a part of your intended planning submission.

You are therefore about to commence the pre-planning stage, and the skills set, expertise, and knowhow required for this specific event will have a particular focus on all of the parts and elements necessary when preparing your planning submission. Completing the application form and submitting your planning documents is actually the last part of the pre-planning process. However, there is a great deal of work to do before you actually make your planning submission. I would suggest, therefore, to keep in mind that managing the pre-planning procedures with a sense of order and organisation is very important so as to achieve the desired planning permission from your local planning authority.

I would also suggest that most of the work involved in pre-planning can

An urban city skyline with a mixture of residential buildings forming the built environment.
(Image by Mikes-Photography)

be undertaken by you managing the process yourself, even if you are a homeowner or self-builder operating on a tight budget. By following the steps set out for you in this four-part series and taking note of the comments and observation made and highlighted throughout (see Chapter 2: 'Your Research & Project Folder'), you will develop the ability to question and decide how best to steer your project through the pre-planning process to the point of making your submission to your local planning authority. For those of us who have lived a life of designing and delivering buildings and developments there is no magic or mystery to it, but there is a process to know about and follow, the essence of which is made available here in this pre-planning book series.

There is perhaps one facet of the pre-planning process that you may not be skilled at regardless of your background, and that is the preparation of the planning drawings. As with the construction process mentioned earlier, you can also adopt the same approach where you may need specific expertise to prepare and complete the planning drawings and any other planning documents. You may not be equipped to prepare or complete the application forms, design and access statements where required, issues relating to sites within a floodplain, etc., for which a particular specialist will be required. By adopting this project management approach, you will maintain overall control of the pre-planning process on your own terms from the very beginning of your development and, of course, make the necessary decisions as part of your self-management remit.

Your objective, therefore, in managing your project either for yourself or on behalf of your client is to recognise the makeup of the built environment within which your site or property is located. You will need to undertake the site research, assess and evaluate the information derived from your research and investigations, develop a visual and contextual awareness of your site or property, and grasp the essence of what site context means for your site's location, which I will introduce you to later (see Chapter 5: 'Built Environment, Context, and Character'). Recognising the location of your site or property for what it is within its built environment or natural environment will form the basis of your site analysis, all of which and more besides is discussed and explained in these *Planning Permission Expertise for Buildings and Extensions* books.

Chapter Two

Getting Organised

Accessing Knowledge

In order to manage your project effectively and efficiently, there are times that call for taking matters by the scruff of the neck. Approaching your project with confidence and determination is possible, of course, when you have access to an information source that will examine the topic in question and assist you in undertaking the tasks involved. Knowledge is power, and being equipped with detailed information which also relates to your particular pre-planning situation will ensure you are better prepared to make more informed decisions. Being more informed about the processes involved for obtaining your planning permission and possible implications relating the construction process later will ensure you minimise your risk, avoid wasting time, and spend your money more appropriately at the correct stages.

The alternative to appointing a qualified architect to manage the pre-planning process for you is to have a qualified architect set out the various actions for you to take yourself. What is important for you to grasp is that within the pre-application process, there are a number of events and actions connected with your project that might have to be done. Equally significant is that there are certain things that must *not* be done, or at least not done at certain times - even avoided with a passion in certain situations. I will highlight and question some of these as we progress through the various activities, particularly when we dive into the constraints (see Book Three: 'Attributes and Constraints'), which I refer to here again later. Constraints can be a minefield, and I will take you through many of them very carefully step by step in a steady man-

Checking what comes first and how to begin the pre-planning process will help you make better decisions.
(Image by jarmoluk)

ner for when you are assessing and eval-uating your site or property.

Irrespective of whether your remit to yourself to manage your own applic-ation or you are appointed to manage the pre-planning process for a client—that is, from zero to obtaining a planning de-cision from your local planning authority—the purpose of this pre-planning book series is to make information available and raise planning issues to help you achieve your objective. There is good reason why you should maintain some awareness of some of the more typical situations, events, and challenges that tend to crop up. Some of these issues are not always apparent or obvious to the layperson, the uninitiated or inexperienced agents, but they can have a profound impact on your project right at the pre-panning stage and even beyond obtaining your planning permission.

I want to make finding out what this pre-planning information is all about as simple as possible. Undertaking this first facet of your project does not have to be a nuisance, a bother, or a bore. Indeed, I find that the project research can be an exciting element of the process because as I find things out, I automatically slot the bits and pieces of information into place in my own mind and set about formu-lating a strategy for the planning submis-sion. Most certainly it keeps you focused, especially when there is money at stake,

Knowing whether your property is in a flood plane and the flood zone defined by the Environment Agency is a typical constraint which must be investigated and assessed for design and development implications
(Image by Don Lodge)

irrespective of whether it is your own or if you are representing your clients' best interests.

Naturally, there are some issues that can emerge which you need to be well prepared for and enlightened about - issues which I have had to deal with during my time in practice. Having been through the process so many times, it becomes somewhat automatic in knowing what to do, when to do it, when not to do something, and what questions to ask; it's almost like having a ready-made checklist in my head every time. The most convenient and realistic way for me to convey this information to you that can serve as your personal reference source - your pre-planning Bible, if you like - is for me to write it down for you.

I consider it significant for you to know what is involved and how certain attributes and constraints connected to your site or property might impact your project at some point during the pre-planning stage. Some of them might even reverberate further into the actual construction process, as I referred to earlier.

It is better you are made aware of these potentially tricky bits and possible risks, upsets, and challenges at the early stages of your project. This will allow you to decide what might be the best action for you to take before you become too committed either financially or in terms of time, to a possible 'red herring'. I would encourage you to focus on each event or situation as they present themselves and set about deciding what is appropriate or affordable for you based on your research and investigations. Avoid investing time

and energy on matters that are distracting and focus totally on the main event: what is required to obtain your planning permission.

Hand-Holding and Access to Information Source

For the self-manager, self-builder, owner-builder, or the less experienced agents about to embark on managing the pre-planning process, there will naturally be a degree of apprehension, but that is not to say managing the pre-planning process cannot be done. Of course it can! I will accept, though, a first-time experience in managing the pre-planning process for a project might be somewhat daunting, but this is only because you are not familiar with the process yet. Through no fault of your own, you do not know the usual stumbling blocks that can crop up, those things that can happen when you are not looking or because you may not know what to look out for or, indeed, where those tricky bits are that can trip you up and cost you time and money, all of which can be painful.

Being able to refer to an information source and a knowledge base that provides the architect knowhow necessary to identify and set out some of these potential difficulties for you is half the battle. By highlighting implications and options available to you in dealing with the more unusual situations and obstacles, certainly more than half the battle is won.

The same will apply when dealing with the process for actually making your planning submission, which in itself is not an insignificant undertaking. This is possible, of course, and online access to your local planning authority is available to everyone. Being able to refer to an information source that is specifically designed to hold your hand and direct you through the various stages of the online application process is naturally a prerequisite if you are to have a real chance of completing the submission process successfully.

Different people will have different reasons for deciding to manage the pre-planning process themselves, but I have found landowners/homeowners, self-builders, and self-managers are the bravest. Being brave, however, is not necessarily the issue; what might be essential for you is managing the project budget with a ruthless determination. Whilst seeking to achieve cost savings might be the primary reason for not engaging a qualified architect or other consultant, you will have to make some budget allowance for having the planning drawings prepared for you if this is outside your own capabilities.It is worth highlighting here, then, the remit of an experienced, qualified architect holding ARB & RIBA status must train for seven years with further years of professional experience. In order for a person to refer to him or herself as an 'architect', they must qualify for registration with the Architects Registration Board (ARB), which usually means successfully completing a minimum of five years of full-time study with two years' work experience in between followed by a final exam in professional practice.

This can usually take an additional year, making a total of eight years from start to finish. Upon acceptance by the

ARB, the architect is then invited to join the Royal Institute of British Architects (RIBA) as a chartered member and entitled to be referred to as a chartered architect. All of this takes commitment and dedication, which many architects shoulder with a big heart because they have a love for what they do.

Architects holding ARB registration are legally entitled to refer to themselves as, and be referred to as 'architects', because the term 'architect' is a legally protected word.

A qualified architect will embrace all design and development aspects and be alert to other possible opportunities associated with your site and property development, whereas a draughtsperson will usually only focus on preparing a set of drawings for you based on what information you provide. That is all you should expect from a draughtsperson.

It is typical for a draughtsperson not to hold any professional indemnity insurance, which is a prerequisite for qualified architects to have in order to ensure compliance with the code of practice set by the ARB. In my experience, builders also never or very rarely hold professional indemnity insurance for any design, permitted development, and planning advice they freely offer and which causes many homeowners, especially, to instruct work to proceed on their site. This often results in illegal building work which is left for the building owner to rectify (see Book Two: 'Avoid Duff Advice').

Setting planning drawings aside for a moment, the next best thing to not actually appointing a qualified architect is to have that expertise at your fingertips. Have a written reference to show you the various steps, what you might need to consider, and what to watch out for and avoid when it comes to having an insight on those tricky bits. Whether you engage with a qualified architect or not, acquainting yourself with the pre-planning process is always healthy. I know from experience this will allow you as the client to function in a more meaningful way by the many relevant and pertinent questions you will be able to ask.

Bear in mind also that functioning as a qualified architect and engaging with clients is a serious business for every architect; it is hugely valued. We are bound by a strict code of practice where inappropriate behaviour or incompetence can render the individual removed from the ARB register at worst or reprimanded at best. Either result will have a significant impact on potential further work opportunities.

I am sure you are mindful enough to realise it is not possible to accommodate over thirty-seven years of experience and practice into a four-book series, but what is possible is to set out a framework for you to identify some of the salient aspects associated with preparing a planning submission for your project or development. These valuable insights will allow you to get a grip on what the fundamentals are: what is involved, what they mean, and what has to be considered and actioned accordingly.

Your Research & Project Folder

Undertaking the management of the pre-planning process means you are about to commence with your research stage, which is where an architect would start. An architect would first set about gathering information about the property. It may consist of an empty site or a building occupying part of the site with surrounding land that perhaps also has some development opportunities. Your property's location and context will dictate what level of development is allowable, and this is what your local planning authority will reference to their planning policies, design guides, development plans, local plans and neighbourhood plans, etc. before they decide to give their decision on your planning application.

This would be a good time for you to start getting yourself organised and to set up your project folder. Your Research & Project Folder(s) will hold everything about your project that you will research and investigate and other information that forms part of the process. As we live in times where technology reigns and we are more conscious of our planet's resources, I suspect you might hold your records and information online or by way of computer storage but you can also keep hard copies, as there are some people who prefer to work this way. Depending upon the nature and size of your project and the number of drawings and documents it will generate, you may decide to separate various sections and create two or three folders, all of which will accommodate your project drawings and documents from the very beginning

to the very end, which is the project handover.

Keeping track of your research and findings relating to your property is an important part of managing your project efficiently. It is important when you are managing the process of moving and directing your project from one stage to the next that you have a means to save and store your information and records easily and that you can access your project information instantly.

My Research & Project Folder contains everything I need to know about my client's property, its location, and its history, including its planning history, of course, which I will examine in some greater detail later. You should also make notes about what else needs to be researched or considered

Your Research and Project Folder allows you to have instant access at all times - at meetings, on site, when leading on design and managing your project. (Image by Sora Shimazaki)

later, and when additional information becomes available, place that in your Research & Project Folder as well. I do all that as I progress the project from work stage to work stage for my client.

I need to be organised and in control of the information flow so I can use it strategically and at the correct time. As my client's architect, I also use my Research & Project Folder when preparing for the following stages of my projects, meaning any time I am considering some design options for the project or specific aspects or areas within the project. I place all my sketches, notes, thoughts, and ideas into my Research & Project Folder within the planning research section so I have all of my information in one place. Notes, design ideas, to-do lists, etc. are all in there. I might even have some thoughts on issues that surfaced

which are connected with building control matters, but that is a separate application process and comes after submitting your planning application. (See Book Four: 'Building Control').

My client may have a request to include some particular item or material they would like to have within their project or some special provision they might be considering later in the project. There may also be matters which really relate to detail design of the construction process. Whilst these items may not necessarily impact on the pre-planning process, I would still record such matters as a client request for inclusion in my project. I usually need to verify these materials and products or special features for suitability and verify costs from suppliers and manufacturers for affordability, or perhaps

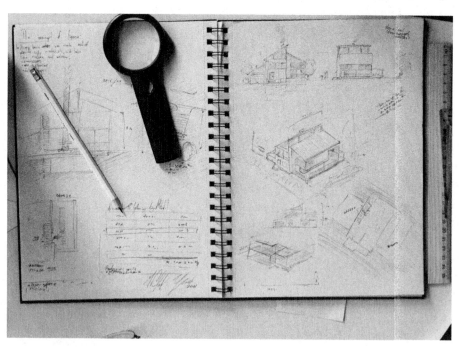

Typical architect's sketch and note book of thinking and ideas
(Image by Tima Miroshnichenko)

Research and Project Folder Contents

PRE-PLANNING & PLANNING SUBMISSION
RIBA Work Stages 0, 1, 2 and 3

1. **Client Matters**
   1.1   Client FUNDER / USER
   1.3   Preparation & Briefing Document   - RIBA Work Stage 1
   1.4   Architects Appointment with Client   - Document

2. **Research & Investigations & Site Appraisals**
   1.1   Neighbourhood Plan or Local Plan Research Information
   1.2   Attributes & Constraints Research & Assessments
   1.3   Existing Services Supply: (Subject for Further Detailed Investigation)
           Below Ground Drainage
           Electricity, Water, Gas Supply
           Telephone & Data Supply
           Other.....

   1.4   Overall Site Measurements   (Topographical Survey Option)
   1.5   Site Photographs
   1.6   Google Earth Images   (Copyright use to be verified)
   1.7   Site Analysis   – Drawings & Documents

   Feasibility   - RIBA Work Stage 2
   1.8   Concept Design Development   – Drawings and Documents
   1.9   Design Options   – Drawings and Documents
   1.9   Indicative Design Solution   – Drawings and Documents

3. **Statutory Authorities**
   3.1   Local Planning Authority
           Pre-Application Submission   – RIBA Work Stage 2
              Indicative Design Solution   (Discussion Purposes with Planners)

   3.2   Building Control   – RIBA Work Stage 3
           Review Building Control Considerations
           Review Potential Asbestos, Soils, and Contamination etc.

   3.3   Final Planning Submission   – RIBA Work Stage 3
           Application Form, Drawings and Documents

DESIGN DEVELOPMENT & CONSTRUCTION
RIBA Work Stages 3, 4 and 5

    3.1   Detail Design Development & Technical Design   – Drawings and Documents
    3.2   Building Control Full Review   – Drawings and Documents

Typical file structure for Research and Project Folder.   (Courtesy of Architect Knowhow Practice)

I need detailed specification information about certain materials and products. I also place that information into my Research & Project Folder under 'materials in readiness' for when I will be under-taking the Technical Design Drawings (RIBA Work Stage 4) and specification. If my client knows they will be flipping (selling) the project after receiving their planning permission decision has been secured, then I will not pay so much attention to the construction process which follows, as it will not impact my client and would not form part of my professional appointment. However, I remain mindful of these aspects because there is always an opportunity for me as an architect to be novated to the new owner as their architect.

My Research & Project Folder, therefore, is a live place; it's my go-to place for my initial thinking on a project, especially surrounding matters relating to planning

3.3	Fire Officer– Drawings and Documents	
3.4	Electricity, Water, Gas	
3.5	Water	
3.7	Communications (Telephone, Data, etc.)	
3.8	Other Statutory Authority	

Architect® Knowhow.

4. Project Drawings
4.1	Survey of Existing Drawings / Photos/ Survey Information
4.2	Architects Project Drawings
4.3	File Record & Register of Issued Drawings
4.4	File Record & Register of Received Drawings
4.3	Other...

5. Design Team & Correspondence
5.1	Project Manager - (Architect or Other)	Emails Received and Issued
5.2	Architect – Lead Design Consultant	Emails Received and Issued
5.3	Quantity Surveyor – (Optional)	Emails Received and Issued
5.4	Structural Engineer	Emails Received and Issued
5.5	Building Services Engineer – (Optional)	Emails Received and Issued
5.6	CDM Coordinator (Health & Safety)	Emails Received and Issued
5.7	Project Specialist Consultants	Emails Received and Issued
5.8.	Architect's - Request for Information Sheets	

5.9	**Specialist Consultants**
	5.9.1 BREEAM Advisor
	5.9.2 Topographical & Measurement Surveyor
	5.9.3 Landscape Architect
	5.9.4 Acoustic Engineer
	5.9.5 Ecologist
	5.9.6 Hydrologist
	5.9.7 Flood Risk Assessment Consultant
	5.9.8 Other

5.10	Designs for Crime Advisor / Secure by Design
5.11	Other......................

6. Project Administration Matters
6.1	DESIGN TEAM MEETING	- Minutes & Notes
6.2	CLIENT MEETINGS	– Minutes & Notes
6.3	PROJECT MEETINGS	– Minutes/ Notes
6.4	Contractor's - Request for Information Sheets	
6.4	Project Programme	
6.5	Project Building Contract Documents	– (Client & Contractor)
6.6	Project Risk Register	
6.7	External Reports (Asbestos, Soils, and Contamination etc.)	

7.   Contractor
7.1	Contractor Tender Process
7.2	Contractor Emails & Correspondence
7.3	Architect's Instructions / Directives
7.4	Certificate of Payments
7.5	....

Typical file structure for Research and Project Folder.   (Courtesy of Architect Knowhow Practice)

when the project is being launched, so all my research information is in there. I will make notes and write down any thoughts I have had about any particular aspect of the project as I go along. I will have some simple sketch ideas there, too, like my first design thoughts as I consider the features and characteristics of the site which I will test later when considering some detail design aspects of the project and developing some concept options. I have this information all in one place where I can easily refer to it at any time.

After this preparation, this information is at my fingertips in one place and ready for when I want to move my project from one stage to the next. It is a living document that reflects events like my pre-planning research, gaining a grasp of the context of the site, developing some concept ideas and finally a design solution, having formal schematic and planning drawing information prepared (informed by my design notes/sketch ideas), and eventually making a planning submission. In other words, I take control of the events and actions by the scruff of the neck, if not by the throat, in order to negate matters being missed or not considered. As it would usually be my remit to manage the construction process following receipt of the planning permission, I would also have a focus on the future building control application, then detailed construction drawings, and eventually move on to the specifications stage which must be prepared for obtaining tender prices from builders. (See Book Four: 'Building Control')

I would ask you, too, to get yourself organised and be ready to take control.

In my career I have been referred to as a 'control freak' at times, but I make no apologies for this, because taking responsibility for my clients' projects is a serious undertaking and necessitates leadership. However, do not confuse control for the sake of it with leadership, because matters relating to planning forms part of an architect's remit as the 'lead consultant'. In your situation, therefore, whether you are leading the pre-planning process yourself or for a client, you will need to take control of events as they occur and lead from the front by way of taking instruction from your client, making decisions, and issuing instructions to others.

I hope I have highlighted sufficient reason for you to create your own Research & Project Folder. I trust you have a good understanding of the importance of managing the information you will be assembling together. You are going to need it throughout the whole of the pre-planning process and beyond, because assuming you will continue project managing your project on-site, you will always be gathering information for that element of the project almost by default. Maintaining your Research & Project Folder will help you to be efficient and keep on top of things. You really do need to keep all of your information organised and in one place. It should always be accessible to you for the duration of your project.

You will have your own particular requirements noted/recorded in your Research & Project Folder, as you may intend to incorporate any simple sketch ideas you have, for example, into the final design solution for your building and your client.

Of course, if you are self-managing the project, all this is very helpful and useful information for whoever you choose to prepare your planning drawings, as you will be able to provide a very clear instruction in this regard. Alternatively, you may decide at some point during the process that this whole pre-planning business is really best left to an expert and elect to appoint a qualified architect. However, having undertaken much of the research yourself is of great benefit and is always an excellent start of a working relationship between an architect and a client. Informed clients are always welcome!

When I discuss appointing your architect (see Book Four), you will see why being well prepared with your information ready at your fingertips is important and valued. You will see why being properly prepared to give and confirm clear instructions to your architect is also important.

Now that we have discussed an overview of the process and the importance of getting organised, we are ready to move on to the next step.

Chapter Three

UK Planning System Overview

General Overview of What Planning and Control Means

The primary focus, however, centres on what your site or property has to offer. By that I mean, apart from achieving the desired planning permission outcome, what can the site or property offer in terms of betterment to the surrounding built environment and the community as a consequence. In essence, this is the thought process required when it comes to considering a planning submission which for some development sites might mean a financial contribution in addition to an appropriate architectural design solution, and for others, such as a simple domestic development, it might mean not creating something that will have a detrimental impact on the surrounding built environment generally and adjoining properties in particular as envisaged by the local planning authority.

The starting point for all of this design thinking and planning consideration for a built environment begins with the pre-planning preparation process which is a process for managing events and ac-

tions that take place before a planning submission is made.

I place a huge emphasis on this part of every project because this is where new buildings and extensions of every shape and size must demonstrate they deserve the right to exist, and a building's right to exist is dictated by two main factors.

In the first instance, it has to be a viable proposition for the property owner or the person procuring the building as it is their money on the table. It must also of course, seek to satisfy the client's ability to pay for the new building or extension and indeed, as the agent, you should assist in determining whether the new building will serve the property owner's intended purpose for the budget available as well as making the client proud of the finished building.

Secondly, when contemplating any new building, building addition, enlargement, or building renovation, you will have to demonstrate that it complies with your local planning authority's planning requirements. Where you have decided to manage this pre-planning process yourself—either as your own self-manager or as an agent acting for your client—

securing that elusive (even illusive, in some instances) planning permission is the big prize, because without it, there is no project.

This book series will be an invaluable tool for individuals currently engaged in preparing planning submissions of all sizes and different levels of complexity. You may be a student of architecture planning or building surveying and construction who has not yet been exposed to the cut and thrust connected with getting a building project off the ground from point zero. Indeed, you may already be providing planning services as an 'agent' for your client, or you may be function-ing as a construction professional and want to know more about the pre-planning process in particular. Understanding the many multifaceted elements, ingredients, alternatives, and trains of thought that are employed when putting a project together from the beginning is not ob-vious to most people and necessitates some level of knowledge, experience, and wherewithal which this book series provides. Of course, there is always room for some common sense as well and a measure of pragmatism if you are to have a reasonable chance of achieving a successful planning permission.

Installation of new steel beams for a modular build-over project. (Courtesy of Architect Knowhow Practice (Image by Author)

Achieving a successful planning permission should not mean deciding on what you would like to achieve, insisting on that objective and anything less is a failure. This is not sensible nor the way the UK planning system works generally. You must bear in mind therefore, planning in the UK is discretionary. As such, preparing a planning submission based on current planning policy and planning guides and making sure your are well prepared to have a mature discussion with the local planning officers at the appropriate time in the process is an important part of the planning process. I cover this later when I introduce the benefits associated with the pre-application process (see 'Typical events timetable earlier'). **See Free Gift on Page 5!**

Most modern countries control urban and rural planning by way of a planning control system, such as Canada, Ireland, New Zealand, the US, Australia, and South Africa, for example. Aspects of this book series may well relate to these jurisdictions in general perhaps and can be used as a reference to ask pertinent and relevant questions accordingly, however, the primary focus here in this book series will relate to the UK planning process.

There may be occasions and reasons for me to refer to the construction stage insofar as it may be relevant to the planning topic under discussion or where your pre-planning preparation process may have a potential impact on the construction process later; for instance, when your planning permission has been obtained. Whilst there are benefits in remaining mindful of certain features and aspects which may impact or influence the construction process, the primary focus here is to assist you in preparing for your planning submission. Thinking ahead like a qualified architect will draw your attention to possible future events, as you will discover in this book series.

The key features necessary to achieve a successful planning submission lie in the preparation of your planning submission, which is referred to as pre-planning. This is a very important process to get right from the beginning in order to achieve a successful outcome. The core elements of what you need to know, such as how and where to start your pre-planning process correctly, are set out for you in this four-part book series.

Understanding the many multifaceted elements, ingredients, alternatives, and trains of thought that are needed when putting a pro-

Houses in Queens New York City. (Courtesy of Pixabay)

ject together from the beginning is not obvious to most people and necessitates some insight and wherewithal which this book series provides. Of course, there is always room for some common sense as well if you are to have a reasonable chance of achieving your planning permission.

School Build-Over Project making use of valuable flat roof as opposed to consuming scarce play space at ground level.   (Image by Author)

When Planning Permission Applies

At this point you are probably wondering to what extent these planning rules and regulations will apply to your particular parcel of land or building. As an agent, naturally you are already alert to the fact that in most cases some form of planning control will apply and a planning permission will be required. Even as a property owner, you are likely aware planning control will apply and your situation, therefore, will necessitate a planning permission for one of the following reasons:

a)

You are seeking to build something new on your land where permitted development does NOT apply (see Chapter 8: 'Planning Permission and Permitted Development').

b)

You are seeking to make some major changes to your building, such as adding a new extension or making significant renovations.

c)

You are seeking to change the existing use of your building or land.

A design solution will always exist for every development site when its context is understood.   (Image by Author)

As a property owner seeking to enhance the value of your piece of real estate, you would reasonably expect that you would be able to develop your land to achieve your particular goals and aspirations. For many development projects this is a reasonable expectation, provided you are not intending to introduce, for instance, a multistorey building into a built environment where the existing surrounding buildings are single storey or double storey at most. That might seem somewhat over ambitious - even unreasonable, perhaps, and most likely out of kilter with the expectations of your local government's development plans for the built environment, other property owners included. The excessive height difference between what already exists against what you might aspire to build - namely a proposal for a multistorey building, for instance - would be in conflict on a number of levels: visually, architecturally, massing/bulk, scale, etc.

This is perhaps an extreme example, but even proposals showing similar or slightly higher roof levels will come under the scrutiny of your local planning authority as well as any interested parties. Even though you are a property owner with intentions to develop your own property which may even be viewed by your local planning authority as a parcel of land ripe for development, you cannot ignore the principles surrounding urban planning or, indeed, architectural design, which you should seek to display as integral to your planning submission.

Similarly, you might be a homeowner or a business owner seeking to add a new addition to your existing building given the large size of your property with surrounding land that is currently unused. The plot ratio of your existing building footprint to the area of available land on your property being sufficiently small, it might well allow some further building footprint to be added as laid down by the planning

A unique approach to roof space creation with architectural design awareness. (Image by Author)

rules. This could be either a new building element, such as extending your existing building, or maybe a totally new detached building on the space available within your site or plot or a combination of both.

Examining your options for your property on another level might be associated with its land use. To cite an extreme example, let us say you now wish to change the existing residential use of your building and land to, say, a night club and hotel or some other form of commercial, certainly nonresidential use. This is often tricky, as it would normally suggest your proposed new use could be deemed to be incompatible with the surrounding residential area in terms of land use as prescribed in the general development plans and the specific neighbourhood plans for your site/land (see Book Two: 'Planning Policy and the Neighbourhood Plan'). In situations where your objective is to change the existing use of the building or land to some-

thing other than what already exists or is allowable, this could very well pose some difficulties in terms of planning. Equally, and depending upon what is set out in the neighbourhood plan for your site location, there may be opportunities to exploit whereby the potential for adding value is a real possibility.

Similarly, your situation might be that your property presently enjoys the benefit of a land use that was permissible in the past, but your local planning authority has since changed the land use requirements for your property and surrounding properties by updating their development and neighbourhood plans. This would suggest that whilst your property presently enjoys the benefit of a particular use, should you seek to extend your property in order to expand the building or land's present use, your proposal might possibly be refused unless your planning submission is so convincing and persuasive that your case for a planning permission is the most likely option for the planners.

The converse is also true in that a change of planning status may be an added bonus for you; you might now have the opportunity to add greater value to your property by this change of planning policy relating to your property. That is another possible welcome bonus, but be prepared for your local planning authority to remind you of this fact (planning gain) and who will be seeking some 'return of profits' by way of a Section 106 agreement or Community Infrastructure Levy (CIL) (see Book Two: 'Section 106 Agreement'). CIL is a planning charge attached to the Planning Act 2008 which came into force in April 2010. It is used as a means for local authorities in England and Wales to access finances to provide development support of their area. You can access more information relating to the CIL from the government website or refer to the link below.

www.planning portal.co.uk

Notwithstanding, there are certain situations and circumstances where the local planning authority employs a measure of progressive thinking and/or recognises when a planning submission has something significant and real to offer. This would be due to the real architectural quality given to the design solution or perhaps the proposed use can offer real benefit to the local community, which would satisfy political masters, or maybe the planning proposal would establish a new visual identity and architectural statement for the area or street which would be encouraged. It might be your proposal introduces new employment opportun-

Planning Authority's discretion employed with planning permission for new hotel with an adjoining residential built environment (Image by Author)

ities and is seen as a much-welcomed opportunity, or it could be a combination of reasons best known to the local planning authority at that time, but they usually refer to their neighbourhood plan for an appropriate reference whenever is suits. That said, it is incumbent upon the applicant and the design team to ensure, as much as possible, to excite the interests of the local planning authority, the local councillors, and planning committee members, all of whom are in the same camp.

You will normally be made aware of your local planning authority's views regarding your planning proposal when you engage with them through the pre-planning process. This is always advisable, as this is an ideal occasion to explore and test the viability and potential of your proposal jointly with your local planning authority (see Book Four). Clearly, should you find yourself blessed with having to deal with such a happy situation, it will place your project potential in a different category altogether, but you also need to recognise that some of the additional value created by this happy event will necessitate a 'return of profits' to the local authority (see Book Two, Chapter 7: 'Creating Added Value').

I was introduced to a new concept of 'return of profits' during my escapades in China while developing project opportunities there. For my China project, it was not only the developer who is expected to adhere to this practice but the architect as well, which meant my practice was required to make a return of profit from the professional fee. This did not sit well with me at all, especially as I was already beaten down on professional design fees

for the commission, just like what happens in the UK when trying to secure a project.

However, the term 'return of profits' was a new phenomenon for me in the way it was presented. But the correlation between the Chinese approach and the UK planning Section 106 approach is very similar in that the developer is required to 'hand back' some of the profit that is realised from the development, which is dependent upon a planning permission being granted by the local planning authority in the first place. The interesting aspect of this type of practice is that for the UK planning system this is legal, apparently. In essence, methodologies employed for extracting some of the developer's benefit, added value, profit, etc. might be different for the different jurisdictions, but the result is the same.

My experience in China boiled down to the fact that, having agreed on professional fees for a multimillion-pound housing and commercial project, there was a requirement for me to return some of the fee (return of profit) to the client, and the client representative was to provide me with the bank details. Needless to say, I was not amused, and neither, indeed, was my Chinese interpreter, who was totally appalled by the notion and viewed this particular meeting as private enterprise at work.

Each site situation is different with its own unique characteristics, challenges, and opportunities that sometimes render some level of change either possible or impossible to make. Planning control, therefore, exists throughout the world so as to organise society and set out national planning laws in the first instance which are then delegated down accordingly.

All property, however, is subject to what the market will sustain, and any added value is derived as a consequence. I am assuming, therefore, that if your property belongs to a homeowner you have already had a discussion with your local estate agent to ascertain what the value of your property might realise should you proceed with your new extension, roof conversion, or separate building, where the land exists. As a homeowner yourself, however, you may not be focused on creating added value as such but more preoccupied with additional living spaces. Equally, I am assuming where your property is of a commercial nature in a city location that you have already obtained some verification as to what the market value will be for your completed apartments or office space.

Delegation of Planning Powers

Much of the UK planning laws of central government are delegated down to the local planning authorities which consist of county councils, city or borough councils, and a collection of district councils. These planning bodies might also have their own separate planning requirements referred to as their byelaws. The location of your site or property will determine which planning body, entity, or authority you will apply to in order to secure your grant of planning permission. Your local planning authority, however, may have to refer back up the chain to

make sure your planning proposal for a given site in a particular village, town, city, or county will not contravene any of the county council planning policies or national planning policies that apply to the UK.

For the private homeowners seeking to extend an existing property or build a new home, the planning process ought to be reasonably simple and straight- forward. In many cases it is straightforward, even painless. For others, however, the processes can result in long, procrastinated deliberations with your local planning authority, their in-house and external consultees, and, of course, those 'interested parties'.

The same planning scrutiny and interested parties' involvement similarly applies to owners of a business premises seeking to increase their work premises. Usually, this is to allow their businesses to function more efficiently and to increase employment opportunities as part of the overall objective.

Interested parties can range from adjoining property owners, neighbourhood groups, conservationists, and groups seeking to save the planet, the local rivers and streams, bat habitats, great-crested newts, your uncle Charlie's pigeon coop, and similar suchlike worthy causes, all of which are commendable and honourable. But in too many instances, they can be detrimental in contributing to the meaning and spirit of planning laws or even offering pragmatic solutions as opposed to recommending the ubiquitous 'no' to every planning submission with a divine passion.

Whether you are contemplating a simple building project or a significant development for your site, there is no escaping the

Managing a planning submission is not always about managing the objection lobby.
(Image by OpenClipart-Vectors from Pixabay)

fact that you will have to navigate your way through these planning processes. For the homeowner, business owner, small-scale builder or developer, planning control can mean the difference between getting on with the job as you would envisage, like many property owners do, or holding your head in your hands for many months - and in some cases years - through frustration and delay.

Planning Change & Zoning

Many countries have now established various structures and procedures for controlling development and regulating how land is used. Indeed, this would include the provision of setting out development rights as well as making provisions for controlling and mitigating against potential environmental impacts new development might pose not only in relation to the site and its surrounding environment but also to the construction process being adopted for the project.

Achieving the most effective planning control system will vary from jurisdiction to jurisdiction. There is a constant demand for planning changes, revisions, adjustments, and all types of tweeting and fiddling at the edges in an endeavour to make the various planning laws and policies of individual jurisdiction more relevant as situations and circumstances dictate. No doubt a measure of the ubiquitous political influence and shenanigans both at national and local level will find its way into the mix. Indeed, the hot debate in the UK at present is the case to abandon its discretionary planning system and utilise some form of regulatory system, something akin to the US zoning system but with some measure of adjustment to accommodate local culture, which is predictable.

Needless to say, the UK planning fraternity have much to say on this proposed planning change and their enthusiasm to surrender their historical long- standing discretionary system is not apparent. This is unsurprising, considering planners within local authorities already possess total power and influence as to what land or property will and will not be developed and how it will be developed, which may not be the case were a zoning system to be introduced to the UK (RTPI, 2020).

Irrespective of whether your property will come under the UK discretionary planning system or some other regulatory system, there will be planning rules you will most probably have to abide by. There will of course always be rules that apply, setting out what you can build and equally setting out what you cannot, unless - which is often the case - the zoning or the planning rules are adjusted for expediency to ac-

Planning

Start typing to filter table...

Undeveloped brownfield at record levels, charity finds
18/11/2021
The amount of undeveloped brownfield land suitable for housing in England has hit a record high, according to new research.

Bucks takes dispute over HS2 lorry routes to co
15/11/2021
Buckinghamshire Council has issued High Court challenges i decisions by the Planning Inspectorate in a dispute over lorry construction.

Shapps outlines planning reforms for better lorr
09/11/2021
Planning reforms will help deliver more lorry parking and bett lorry parks, the secretary of transport has said.

Government must engage with councils on clim
29/10/2021
MPs have called for the Government to 'immediately' begin w councils on setting out their role in reducing carbon emissions

Councils selected for £1m digital engagement tr
26/10/2021
Thirteen local areas are to share £1m of Government funding initiative to boost public engagement with the planning proces digital innovations.

Report calls for communities to be given more p planning
25/10/2021

Major planning changes on the cards to facilitate Growth Local Government Planning, (n.d.) & In research from Skopeliti (2021) .

Announcing the planning bill, the government had pledged it would create "simpler, faster procedures for producing local development plans, approving major schemes, assessing environmental impacts and negotiating affordable housing and infrastructure contributions".

Ministers had aimed to use the loosening of planning regulations, which have been in place since 1947, to boost home ownership in areas of rising Conservative support in northern England and the Midlands, as well as using post-Brexit freedoms to "simplify ... environmental assessments for developments".

However, the Lancashire, Liverpool city region and Greater Manchester branch of the CPRE charity, which lobbies to protect the countryside, described the planned reforms as an "utter disaster", with chair Debra McConnell saying: "We will see a lot more houses on greenfield land and in areas of outstanding natural beauty. The people in the north of England need these green spaces for their wellbeing."

As well as criticism from countryside campaigners who say the changes would result in "rural spread", the government has been condemned for failing to put forward legislation to improve regulation of social housing. Grenfell United, which represents the bereaved and survivors of the 2017 tower block disaster, said it was "deeply let down" at the failure to "redress the balance of power between social housing tenants and landlords" in the Queen's speech, where the planning reforms were first mooted.

Over the past five years, social housebuilding has averaged below 6,500 new homes a year in England, according to Shelter, while there are 1.1 million people on waiting lists.

commodate a proposed development for your particular parcel of land (Merriam, 2004).

Consequently, as a property owner or one managing the pre-planning process on behalf of your client, you should generate an understanding of what planning options exist for the property and whether you can avail of the permitted development route or, given the nature of what you intend, if a planning submission would be more appropriate. Permitted development rights mainly apply to houses but not to flats or maisonettes. Permitted development rights cal also apply to commercial properties but these tend to be more complex but certainly possible. Having a clear understanding of what options exist will assist you in ascertaining the most cost-effective and time-efficient route to achieve your preferred planning objective.

Being alert to some of the typical potential pitfalls that can crop up during the pre-planning process will keep you focused and help you to make more appropriate decisions for your project, which really start at this pre-planning stage. Having an idea of what options might be available during this initial stage is vitally important in order for you to progress through your pre-planning process as efficiently as possible. In fact, you are carrying out your due diligence to achieve the best possible planning solution for your property, just like you would do when purchasing a piece of real estate.

It is easy to feel somewhat bamboozled and maybe intimidated by it all, especially if this is your first development project or if you are somewhat inexperienced. I would ask you to set aside any confusion or apprehension you might have at this time relating to all the planning laws, byelaws, and planning policies, because you do not need to know everything about everything. Much of what you will need to deal with for your project will come out in the wash as you methodically progress through the various stages of preparing your application. In essence, you only need to know what is relevant to your particular development for your given site in your particular location. Focus on that alone, and focus on what questions you should be asking yourself.

The main feature to bear in mind is that within the UK, the planning system is based on a discretionary system which indicates your approval is granted or refused at the discretion of your local planning authority. You do, of course, have the right to lodge an appeal against a planning refusal or conditions attached to your planning permission where you might deem the same to be onerous (see Book Two: Planning Conditions and What They Mean'). Preparing an appeal, however, is another specialism and not for discussion in this book series.

The US enjoys the benefit of a regulatory system, which has its own advantages and foibles, and design professionals there, too, appear to have much to complain about. But what is attractive about it is the 'as of right' concept attached to the zoning principle which at least offers some level of guarantee and certainty for building some type of building, as opposed to potentially building nothing or 'You will build what we want you to build' as prescribed by the UK discretionary planning system.

Notwithstanding the differences between the discretionary and regulatory systems, there are many similarities when approaching a development project whether it is located within the UK or other jurisdictions. Many of the actions that have to be taken are similar and the approach for having planning issues resolved also follows a similar pattern, albeit the process for dealing with planning matters will differ somewhat.

What are the Planning Options

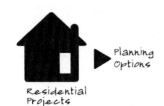

Residential Projects

Planning Options ▶

Planning Permission
Prepare and make a Planning Submission

OR

Permitted Development Rights
Prepare and make an Application for a Certificate of Lawfulness

Non Residential Projects

Planning Option ▶

Planning Permission Only
Prepare and make a Planning Submission

Certain residential projects can avail of Permitted Development Rights to circumvent having to apply for planning permission. (Diagram by Author)

Stop Press Item!

As I was happily making progress editing this first book of the series, the news broke. Lo and behold, the UK government decided to withdraw their intention to introduce planning reform. The hopes and dreams of many within construction and many, I suspect, in the architectural profession have been shattered by this latest decree. The media reported the cancelling of planning reform was brought about by the Conservative Party losing a by-election to the Liberal Democrats who, with the voting public being hyper about a 'developers' charter' and a 'planning free-for-all', would bring ruin and damnation to us all.

Did I not mention there are occasions where political influence is brought to bear?

That said, the manner in which permitted development rights are exploited to circumvent planning control in some instances warrants close monitoring (see Book Two: 'Research and Investigations: Planning and Permitted Development').

Chapter Four

Leading the Pre-Planning Process

Self-Managing

In most cases - that is, where planning permission is required - no building work can legally commence on the jobsite yet. Having some appreciation for and understanding of the processes and procedures connected with making a planning submission or an application for a Certificate of Lawfulness is a prerequisite to completing your project with some level of competency and efficiency.

Self-managing your own building project is no doubt a more intense challenge, but if you feel you have the ability to manage or perhaps are blessed with some building and construction knowledge already, then you are indeed in a very good place. Being equipped to this degree will not only assist you in achieving better value for your money but will also reduce and

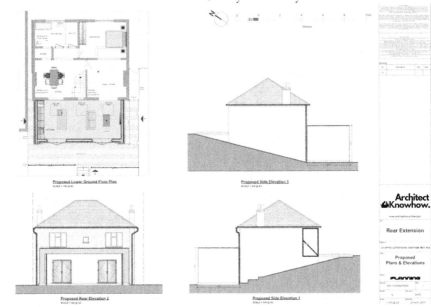

Typical Pre-Application drawing information for discussion purposes with local planning authority prior to final planning submission.
(Courtesy of Architect Knowhow)

negate much of the anxiety, frustration, and delays that can occur, primarily because you are in total control of the processes and procedures involved. However, for some, taking on the pre-planning and preparation of a planning submission is a matter they would prefer to delegate to someone more familiar with the preparation and application process. In this case, you might well consider appointing someone who will manage the pre-planning process for you. This person is referred to as 'the agent' on the planning application form and is referred to as such by your local planning authority. Further reference is made to employing a qualified architect or a draughtsperson as your agent later.

The primary ingredient that needs to be grasped from the beginning, however, is recognising the importance attached to preparing your UK planning submission. This is often referred to as 'pre-design' or 'pre-planning', which embraces all of the events and actions that should take place before you finally make your planning submission. This would include matters surrounding your project generally: your site research, investigations, and assessments together with developing some concept ideas. Your concept ideas can be simple sketch plan layouts and diagrams, preferably to scale to make them more meaningful, in order to verify the viability of your project and to satisfy yourself that a planning permission for what you intend is indeed achievable. There is not much point in submitting a planning proposal that is not sustainable and makes no sense in both planning and economics terms.

Preparing your planning submission is based on the research and investigation work that needs to be undertaken in order to ensure your submission to your local planning authority is presented in a comprehensive and competent manner. In this regard, the findings from your site research will form the very essence of what goes into understanding your site in terms of context, character, and its surrounding built environment and will consequently inform and influence the final architectural design solution.

Acting as your own client or on behalf of your client, you will lead the preparation of planning documents which will include drawings, all of which must be prepared and completed correctly before you actually make your planning submission to your local planning authority. It is very important, therefore, for you to grasp the concept that information about your site or your existing building on a site is key when seeking to achieve your planning permission. In fact, your site and everything about or relating to your site forms the very essence for developing an architectural design solution.

The thrust of highlighting these aspects is because prior to you formally making your planning submission, comprised of all your research to which your planning proposal refers, you are in an ideal situation to seek pre-planning advice from your local planning authority. You would be well advised to obtain pre-planning advice from your local planning authority by way of a pre-application submission. In essence, this is a process whereby you obtain a formal opinion from your local planning authority as to the likelihood

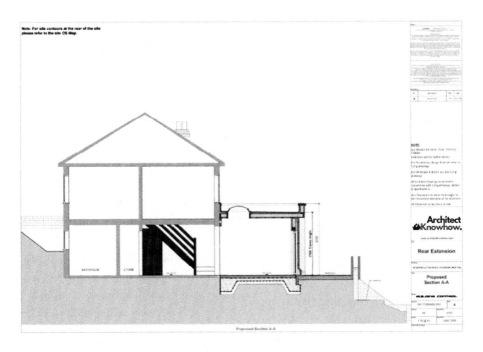

Typical cross section through the site and building to show varying levels
and the new rear extension in relation to the existing building.   (Courtesy of Architect Knowhow)

Minimum drawing information
for a simple single storey rear extension

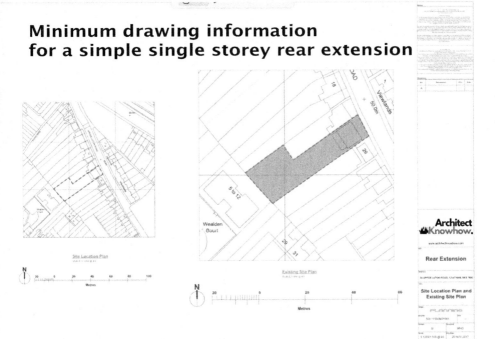

of them granting you a planning permission (see 'Pre-Application Process').

Understanding what should take place before you make your formal planning submission to your local planning authority is a key feature of your planning strategy. This will apply whether your property asset is located within a city in Lancashire, a village in Suffolk, a neighbourhood in Scotland, or a village in Wales. This is fundamental information that is really a must-have as part of your armoury.

I fully understand the excitement extending your home brings to you and your family, or if you have a business premises you may encounter the temptation to discuss your goals and ambitions with adjoining property owners just to get a handle on what their responses would be. However, I would suggest that is not a wise action to take and should be avoided at this time (see Chapter 7: 'Preparing a Planning Submission').

Pre-Application Process

There are naturally differences between a simple domestic extension and a project which is nonresidential or more substantial. There are some domestic extensions not catered for under permitted development rights, and therefore making a submission for a planning permission is the only option available. A planning submission for a typical domestic extension, for instance, will not usually necessitate a barrage of supporting information and planning documents, as these are normally simple and straightforward.

However, there are occasions where even domestic extensions and conversion projects can generate a hype of controversy and are blown up into a mega project out of nothing except, perhaps, personal interest. I experienced this situation for a simple residential project consisting of seven town houses where my client sought to clean up and substitute a waste disposal site (a brownfield site, note) located within a London suburb surrounded on the perimeter by two- and three-storey housing apart from the two site access points. Needless to say, even before a planning submission was made it hit the local media. Local politicians engaged for their votes and indeed every local objector within a radius of five miles was recruited for the objection campaign, who sought to promote the land as an 'inner-city meadow' use instead. Whilst the client was happy to sell the land for that specific use, neither the council nor the objectors were prepared to finance that notion. Common sense prevailed in the end, where a planning permission for housing was eventually granted, but the moral of this story is: Do not discuss your development intentions with adjoining property owners, as word can travel with haste.

I always make it a policy to promote the pre-application process to my clients for certain residential projects and especially in relation to nonresidential or commercial developments. It is an ideal opportunity for the client to obtain a heads-up as to the viability of the proposed development prior to making a formal planning submission. Whilst there is a certain amount of design and preparation of work required in order to present a sensible proposal, this is usually an amount of work sufficient to be able to explain what it is you are proposing. The pre-application process does, however, negate the need to proceed to a formal planning submission, where the formal response resulting from the pre-application process suggests a refusal is the more likely outcome were you to proceed with a formal planning application (see Chapter 4: 'Making a Pre-Application').

Taking advantage of the pre-application advice process with your local planning authority is always Recommended. (Image by Malachi Witt)

I usually invite my clients to also attend the pre-application meeting with the local planning authority. This is an excellent opportunity for the client to obtain a firsthand account of the planning officers' views and mood surrounding their development goals and aspirations for the site, the location, and the surrounding built environment. It is also a valuable opportunity for me to explain and discuss the objectives of the project, the thinking employed together with how I referenced ('Policies, Neighbourhood Plans, & Design Guides') the design solution for the particular site, location, and context. The pre-application meeting also allows me to measure the mood and present some alternative solutions should that be necessary (Plan B can save the day).

Lastly, I also seize the occasion to ask the planning officers to provide me with a list of the information they would expect to accompany the planning submission as part of their formal response to my pre-application. The pre-application process will conclude by way of a formal response from the planners, the basis of which will reflect what was discussed and agreed upon at the meeting and pave the way for making any adjustments to the final design solution, completing the preparation of any other planning documents, and then making a formal planning submission.

At the end of your pre-application process, your final submission, therefore, represents the culmination of your planning research together with the preparation of your planning documents that will be required in order to achieve the desired planning result. In essence, in order to make an appropriate planning application there is a process to follow, at the end of which will result in a set of planning documents that forms your planning submission.

Project Costs and Residential Budgets

For homeowners and property owners fortunate enough to have a healthy budget for your project, you may be of a mind to appoint an architect from the very beginning (see Chapter 2: 'Hand Holding - Information Source and Architect Knowhow'). This will allow you to get on with your life - to a point, perhaps. I have found, however, that most clients still devote time and mental energy to what is happening as a natural course of events, primarily because it is their money that is in the pot and usually at risk, in my experience! I am aware that experienced commercial clients and public authorities know the value a qualified architect can bring to the table and they also have their finger on the pulse, either from their own hand or that of a client representative who they appoint to manage their interests while they get on with other projects.

Your architect will no doubt guide you through much of the processes and actions that have to be completed and indeed undertake some of the work for you if required. However, if your project is of a smaller scale, such as a self-build/owner-build project, you may be obliged to ensure every pound and penny of your money is only spent on what you are not able to undertake yourself. In that case, then I suspect you intend to undertake whatever is possible yourself.

Depending on how you evaluate your own skills, you might envisage managing the pre-planning process is possibly for you. The preparation of your planning submission is the first item on the agenda for any new project; whether it is a new build or a renovation, you will need to adopt a similar approach when managing the pre-planning process yourself. Whether or not you do decide to appoint an architect to manage the pre-planning process for you will incur professional fees.

These project costs will come about with appointing an architect who will usually manage the pre-planning process for you. This will include the preparation of all drawing information in readiness for your pre-application and final planning submission, ultimately.

Should you choose not to appoint an architect, you will still have to have your drawing information prepared for your pre-application process and, again, for your final planning submission. If this is not a skill you possess yourself, there are draughtspersons who provide a drawing service, but do bear in mind that is what it is: a drawing service, usually without any measure of in-depth design prowess.

In *The Planning Submission*, which is the fourth book in this pre-planning series, I discuss project costs in more detail. I refer specifically to planning costs and building control costs more specifically, primarily because too many homeowners tend to believe the only costs associated with achieving a planning permission lies with the preparation of 'planning drawings'. This is not always the case if your project is in any way different from a simple single-storey rear addition referred to earlier.

I also discuss construction costs together with other potential costs that may be attracted to your project. Clearly, the construction cost is the big-ticket item, and I outline why it is important to follow a proper tender process so as to achieve a 'like-for-like' cost comparison from builders. I also explain why it is important to consider your specification carefully to ensure you have included what you need and want and that you can indeed afford the project.

The processes and topics discussed in this book series will provide you with a comprehensive account of the more typical issues that you are likely to come across. At the same time, you will be introduced to a mindset of thinking to help you ask relevant and pertinent questions about your specific project as a natural part of the process as well as when you should appoint professional help to make your collaboration with your architect more meaningful.

In the next chapter I refer to topics which, for the local planning authority, form a very significant element of your intended planning submission. Very often, planning submissions are made with the skimpiest of drawing information and almost always no reference to the site, its location, and what is happening around it, thereby leaving it to the local planning authority to make a decision almost in a vacuum. Candidly, this situation can often result in a refusal.

Every planning submission, therefore, needs to be explained as to why a grant of planning permission is appropriate. Referencing your design solution to the surrounding built environment, its context, and its character are ingredients for every planning submission to include as a prerequisite.

An alternative architectural design approach to an existing street scene is always possible   (Image by Author)

Chapter Five

Built Environment, Context and Character

Introduction

We often hear mention of the built and natural environments as places and spaces, how they relate to our well-being and provide environments which enrich human lives - or at least that is the theory. Built environments define cultures and buildings, too, providing a means to identify a particular city or a place at a glance. Indeed, the built environment especially touches the lives of many in a number of ways and different to those whose lives are spent in rural locations where the natural environment is predominant.

Essentially, the clue is in the word 'built', where inner cities, urban, and suburban environments are determined by the density of buildings and their occupation, as are towns and villages, albeit to a different level of intensity. As well as external environments, buildings are also designed to provide internal environments which allow us to live and work and enjoy recreation in a modern world. There are also other facilities and

Shaping a new built environment with the Burj Khalifa in Dubai   (Image by Jeff Tumale)

City built environments with buildings and bridges.
(Image by Richard Lee)

spaces purely for the enjoyment of human recreation activity within them, and some level of the natural environment might be introduced by way of parks, trees, and plants.

We tend to spend a great deal of our time in buildings, whether it is our own homes or place of work, but in all cases the management of our built environment is controlled by planning regulations. The planning regulations dictate how tall buildings will be, how they must be laid out and arranged, and establish the required space between them. There is no set formula for providing the ideal city or town layout, and every newly designed town or city that has sprung from a landscape hailed perhaps as the next great built environment solution for human occupation has always appeared to be a great experiment for some, but I have yet to be acquainted with the perfect utopia.

Some cities and towns have a more historic reference by the way the place has evolved throughout the centuries, and for some planning authorities, any new development will be influenced accordingly on a number of design levels.

Not all development creates new buildings, as many development projects consists of repurposing existing buildings that

distribution systems that allow us to function within our buildings like water, electricity, gas, and telephone services, all of which require specialised structures above ground and service facilities below ground. Our built environments are also made up of roads, flyovers, and bridges which facilitate our movements in and around the places and spaces we identify as the built environment.

Our built environments also accommodate open spaces - spaces between buildings which accommodate roads for our transport systems and pavements for human movement. We might also enjoy the benefit of open

Open spaces within built environments
(Image by Karolis Vaiciulis)

are no longer fit for the purpose they were originally built to fulfill.

Many projects of this nature do not interrupt or change the existing built environment in a material way, and any planning permission required might be for a change of use. Others do necessitate a change to the existing built environment, for which a planning permission will also be required. Most people will not be directly connected with major building projects except where a proposal under consideration is close to their 'backyards', as it were. And with that,

all hell can break loose because it can become personal - *very* personal, indeed, as my client's waste disposal site became very personal for a number of surrounding property owners.

In the main, most people might be more interested in a development activity located immediately adjoining their property. In the majority of cases, this tends to be an adjoining property owner expressing views about whether your proposed new building or extension will diminish the value of their property as they might understand it, which may be a residential or nonresidential property.

The adjoining property owner's assertion may be real and valid, or it might be a perceived claim without any supporting evidence. Evidence or not, it is irrelevant, because the whole process will become a matter for your local planning authority to deliberate over and decide whether your proposed new building or extension will have a material impact on its built environment and your adjoining properties. There is one exception to this, of course, and that is the scourge of ill-considered permitted development extensions for certain residential projects. They tend to generally be devoid of any architectural design input or reference to the surrounding built environment and adjoining properties in particular, over which there is no planning control.

Let us examine, then, the places where we live and work as environments. Because we tend to live and work in buildings, the term 'built environment' thus has a more direct meaning. The precise location of your property within a particular environment is naturally more relevant to you, as it is more personal, as are the spaces and buildings which surround your property occupied and owned by others. This is especially important to consider if you are contemplating some development by way of a new building or extending an existing building.

The built environment is often referred to, in a global sense, as our towns and cities and places where we live and work. An individual building or parcel of land that you own is usually examined in planning terms in relation to the adjoining properties as being part of the immediate environment in the first place.

Our immediate built environment sets the mood of the place, which will relate to us more readily and directly because we are familiar with it. We know how it works and what makes it tick by the functionality of the place and the people who occupy it. It gives us a sense of place and belonging, as we tend to have a good grasp of what is happening in our own vicinity. Buildings of any description and their surrounding

505C - A residential environment in South London (Photo by Author)

Typical UK housing development creating new suburban built environments located within a wider built environment. (Image by Alan Walker)

spaces create streetscapes. Streetscapes that are located a little distance from us or where we do not have a direct connection and cannot see do not have the same meaning as the streets or roads that we actually live on or collect our groceries from or go to have a haircut at our local barber. Our immediate environment tells us about the place in which we live or work or where we spend time at recreation. Our built environments, then, tell us the way we might feel about the place as we become familiar with it, for better or for worse.

Beyond our own immediate environment a wider environment exists, all of which links up in many different ways either by a combination of more buildings or open spaces like a city park, village green, a river, or even a lake, perhaps. The degree to which our immediate and wider built environments connect or not is not only visible to us on the ground but is usually referred to in some way in the neighbourhood plan or local plan, the ultimate arbiter for planning decisions - or so we are led to believe. Having sight of these from your local planning authority is a

prerequisite for any new development whether it is a totally new building or extending an existing building. Gaining an understanding of what your local planning authority will expect is the next prerequisite, as they will refer to the neighbourhood plan or local plan when assessing your planning submission.

I have often been told by my domestic clients they want to achieve a design solution that has sympathy and recognises the adjoining properties. I suppose the crux of what I am being told is to design a solution that will not upset the adjoining property owners in order to avoid objections. Deciding when to approach the adjoining property owners has historically been a hit-and-miss endeavour for many homeowners, primarily because it is almost impossible to judge what level of response you will attract. I referred to this topic earlier and I discuss this very matter in more detail in Book Two, Research and Investigations, when I refer specifically to keeping your project private and the reasons for doing so. Consequently, in this book it is sufficient for me to highlight that there

A 2016 residential development creating a new built environment in the London Borough of Greenwich (Image by Author)

is a correct time to have a conversation with anyone about your intended project, and this process has to be managed.

In discussing their project objectives, my clients clearly demonstrate some level of awareness of the built environment and what that means. It is sufficient to know that by introducing a new physical entity, it can have an impact. Many point out to me also they want to achieve a design solution which not only enhances their property aesthetically and functions well for their specific needs but equally will not diminish the adjoining owners' property as a consequence. They recognise that paying a professional consultant's fee is part of their overall project cost. Clients of this calibre recognise the professional's design fee as an investment rather than an unwelcome cost and recognize, too, that a planning permission is never guaranteed, irrespective of whether you have the blessing of the adjoining property owners or not.

Typical urban built environment where a combination of residential and employment Activities coexist. (Image by Author)

You may decide not to employ the design skills and expertise of a qualified architect but opt instead for the input of a draughtsperson to act as your agent and prepare your planning drawings. In this case, you will have to accept the planning drawings will very often be in isolation of any meaningful relationship to the building's context or character and you then will have to assume responsibility by default for deciding what your new building or extension should look like and how it will fit into the surrounding built environment.

Consequently, being alert to what already exists is an important element in seeking to ensure your new building recognises what is actually happening architecturally.

Of course, your property might be a parcel of land with no building on it or a property which consists of land and a building. Either way, it has a connection to a built environment which surrounds your site or property and that, in actuality, becomes your terms of reference for architectural context. In other words, your site or property can never be seen in isolation,

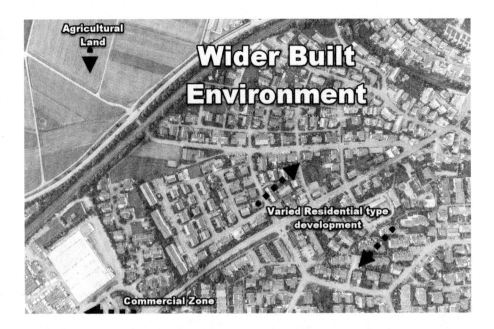

Agricultural Land

Wider Built Environment

Varied Residential type development

Commercial Zone

A wider built environment within which separate immediate built environments exists
(Image by StockSnap)

as it is always connected visually and physically by the buildings, open spaces, trees, bridges, etc. which make up its built environment. Similarly, you must also remain mindful of the existing use of your site location and alert should your planning submission seek to secure a change of that use. Your local planning authority will expect compelling reasons for them to grant your planning permission - unless your proposal meets with their goals and aspirations at the time, all of which is at their discretion.

Built Environment & Context

You now have an understanding as to what a built environment consists of: buildings, open spaces, and supporting infrastructure where urban designers and town and city planners apply their influence on the art of architecture. Essentially, our towns and cities consist of a mix of physical entities, all of which have three-dimensional form, and they all occupy a footprint on the ground and space in the air. But what is it that makes these arrangements of buildings, open spaces, and structures work successfully - or not, as the case may be? There is an array of academic argument and debate as to the rights and wrongs of how and why our urban built environments should be designed in a particular way where context is used as a design tool in architecture (Panda, 2020).

It is not my intention to smother you with rarefied architectural language and terminologies or to adopt a highbrow take when explaining the architectural context and character of a place; that is not the purpose of this pre-planning book series. However, I do want to introduce you into a mindset of having a simple appreciation of the way your neighbourhood and built environment is made up, the way it works, and the way it might be described by your local planning authority.

As an agent or one self-managing the pre-planning process yourself, it is important to have a general appreciation for and sense of the three-dimensional form of your surrounding built environment. Being able to discuss ideas and options relating to the building form and surrounding spaces and adjoining properties in a sensible, pragmatic way with your local planning authority is a valuable attribute to have.

On the other hand, if you are acting on behalf of your client as an agent, the ability to interact and engage in meaningful discussion with the local planning authority on design specifics associated with the built environment is a positive indication that you are mindful of the existing built environment's formation. This expertise can allow you to explain that what you are proposing is a good fit and precisely why in architectural and planning terms. As an architect acting as the agent for your client, it is incumbent upon you to set out your reasoning as to why a planning permission should be granted, taking all

planning matters and policy into consideration.

With regard to the built environment and context, I want to highlight some obvious factors and physical features that come into play which, when examined and assessed together, make up the essence of what is under consideration in planning terms. These physical factors and features might be the surrounding buildings, but they can also be trees, a nearby river or lake, or open space; the gradient of a road or your actual site are seen as pivotal in some respects

A built environment within a town centre where the mood of the place is defined by its buildings and Spaces. (Image by Kai Bossom)

by your local planning authority. You neighbourhood plan or local plan will enlighten you as to the situation in this regard, and at your pre-application meeting with the local planning authority they will certainly bring this fact to your attention together with other relevant matters.

Consider if your property is located within a rural environment. Perhaps the view from your site is a primary factor and, indeed, your reason for wishing to purchase the site in the first place. A particular view might be a key feature for your adjoining property owner also, and you proposing a new building in a particular position which interrupts this important view might give grounds for a legitimate objection. You should bear in mind, however, that even if you can demonstrate the said view is not sacrosanct in planning terms, other reasons and objections tend to erupt in a bid to maintain the status quo, and it would be wise for you to consider what these possibilities are beforehand so they can be managed.

All of these features and events have a part to play in formulating a design solution where identifying the context of your site or property is fundamental in presenting a planning submission to your local planning authority. The skill and expertise of a qualified architect is employed for this purpose, where they will demonstrate the important aspects have been considered and catered for within the final design solution.

In essence, there are different types of built environments and each has its own specific context, character, and personality. For example, there is an inner-city environment, urban or suburban, and rural, as I mentioned earlier. Architectural context helps to describe the character of a built environment by giving meaning to the

A vacant development site within an existing streetscape ·
(Image by Author)

place where a building or buildings have a significant presence and plays a major part in the formation of the built environment. This is expressed by the building's features, the building's parts, and by the way these are referenced to its surroundings (see Chapter 5: 'Context Appreciation').

For instance, buildings making up a built environment could be an apartment block, a town house, or a detached, semi-detached, or terraced house. It could even be a mix of different types of properties within the same vicinity. Equally, the environment could be business premises or commercial buildings of some sort, and there could be a mix of different types of properties with various functions all contributing to the local and wider economies in their own specific, unique way.

Whatever the building type is, whether it is a residential building or nonresidential, it will still have its own physical features and elements which makes your building or site what it is. Therefore, you cannot consider your site or building in isolation of what is happening around it; that is simply choosing to be ignorant of what exists.

Buildings of all types and functions and other structures of all types and function - such as a bridge, a monument, or a communications tower - are physical entities with a physical presence and contribute to the community. Thus, they must justify their place accordingly. They command a footprint on the ground and space in the air which all make up this three-dimensional composition we refer to as the built environment. Whatever your property will consist of, it will have to add and contribute to this built environment and community mix as well, which is a constantly evolving entity.

Context Appreciation

The next topic I want to refer to is context - architectural context, that is, as we tend to view, compare, and evaluate our own property in context with what is happening and going on around us in our immediate built environment. Architectural context has a focus on values and design principles and indicates the meaning of the place.

We might view our own property with particular scrutiny in terms of the factors and features that might exist and consider how it all compares with adjoining properties in the first instance. Initially, therefore, there is good reason to focus on the site or property itself, as this is where the main action will take place with regard to the remodelling of the site or building and how your new design proposal will add value to the built environment.

The significant aspect to grasp with architectural context is the fact that you are examining and assessing physical entities and human activity that already exist; you seek to decide how your proposed design solution will fit in with that which already exists within its immediate built environment. Context appreciation does not necessarily have a concentration on the built form or arrangement of buildings, as it also relates to what the building might be used for or should mean in terms of providing employment or serving the immediate community is some significant way.

Beyond your immediate environment, you should also seek to evaluate your property or site with other properties and buildings that are not so directly connected, perhaps, either visually by the way they look or physically by their presence and function. Understanding their presence or the architectural influence they may have by the way they complement the place visually and how they they fit in - or don't, as the case may be - is a key indicator when considering a design solution for your property.

Of course, certain streets or roads might have a collection of properties that are the same, even identical in some instances, and nothing has changed since they were first built. Perhaps you may be the first looking to introduce a measure of change with the new extension or a new building you are now considering. With regard to your planning submission, you may wish to ask yourself: What potential will your new building or extension bring to what already exists? To what degree will your new building and its function/use contribute to the existing context based on how it already works?

For further clarity, let me cite an example. For instance, the manner in which family houses are built in current times is literally generations apart from those that constituted a family house back in Georgian times. It would be odd indeed to build a modern-style house within the middle of a row of pure Georgian houses. It would be peculiar, too, to build a truly Georgian house within a street or road consisting of contemporary-style houses which reflect current times. Both really would be out of context and in many ways out of character with what is happening or going on in the place generally. They would be considered to be out of context because they are different properties built for different life-styles and at different times; in fact, they are many generations apart. So, let me expand on context a bit further, and I promise to keep it simple.

Contextualism or contextual architecture is a process in which a structure (your building, which is a three-dimensional physical entity) is designed in response to its specific environment for a specific era with a specific requirement. This could be an inner-city street or area, as we would identify with today; an urban, suburban, or rural environment; or a natural environment, if that is where your property is located.

Rather than being primarily an architectural style, which is something else (see Chapter 5: 'Character and Style in Buildings'), contextualism can be seen as a set of values or ingredients representing a society and design principles that are incorporated into a building's architectural design for a given environment at a given time.

In other words, the surrounding physical three- dimensional context is used as a design reference to formulate a design solution for your new building or your new addition to an existing building on a specific site in a specific location within its specific built environment.

In an architectural sense, context gives meaning to parts of a building by reference to its surroundings, including other buildings, their function, their character, and their style. This does not mean the agent is required or expected to copy and paste the design details and features of adjoining buildings, however, as that would never allow architecture to progress. Besides, architecture is more than that.

Context, then, not only refers to the surrounding buildings by their form, mass-

Extended a Victorian terrace is always possible with an appropriate architectural design solution and design principles adhered to.   (Image by Author)

ing, and density but also includes other physical and natural factors and features. For example, it may answer how a new building might address the height and form of an adjoining building or the proportions of existing buildings forming the streetscape.

Context also refers to usage of the building within the built environment and whether a change of use would be deemed compatible with what already exists is also considered.

The buildings referred to here have a historical context given their location and their proximity to a Royal Park. These factors and features can be analysed, adapted, and adopted to integrate the design for the new building into its current context. The image above shows how a typical example of a terrace of town houses of one architectural style is continued with two new houses of a later style that is added to that streetscape. It is a simple example of how the mood and feel of the place is retained without slavishly copying every architectural detail and feature of the existing

houses from a different period and culture. In essence, the design solution here respects the existing architectural context by adhering to essential design principles where the proportions are replicated within a modern architectural design solution. Context, of course, does not only relate to heritage schemes but forms the essential reference for any architectural design solution for any given period.

Now we are going to take look at dealing with actual details and features. In addition to the actual form, shape, size, and massing of a building as a physical entity, there are then particular features of a building or group of buildings which symbolise and depict the character and style of a particular period. Examples include the Georgian window of the Georgian period (1714 to 1830), a mansard roof which became popular in the early 17th century, or an Art Deco building synonymous with the 1930s.

Context is derived from what already surrounds the existing site location whether it is city, urban or rural. (Image by Nick Fewings)

The image above is a simple example of context, but equally, there are other features not associated with a building which also lend context to a place. The bend of an adjacent river, protected trees, a listed building, or proximity to an open space like a park, the countryside, a lake, or even a particular road are all features and factors which provide architectural context to the built environment.

Architecturally, there are some significant elements to be considered, and by working your way through this pre-planning book series you will have a better sense of how to embrace these ingredients and incorporate them as part of your design solution. You may be engaged in managing the pre-planning process yourself and feel comfortable issuing instructions as to how your design proposal is to be prepared by way of drawings for planning submission

purpose. On the other hand, a trained architect will manage this with great skill and care, just like a skilled surgeon will approach his patient's surgical operation. There is a difference, of course, in managing the pre-planning process yourself but delegating this work to a qualified architect is a better option (Gaine, 2021).

On another level, sociocultural, sociopolitical, and socioeconomic factors will similarly lend some context to the place by the manner in which the land or building is to be used or has been used in the past, or perhaps how it should be used in the future. Maybe for political reasons more than planning, there is a preference for the context of the place to be changed or altered somewhat. Your planning proposal for your site location with a different function lends itself to that objective, which can sometimes be an unexpected bonus. However, there will be a 'payback' expected by the local planning authority by way of a 106 Agreement (see Chapter 3: 'UK Planning System Overview'). Irrespective of any unexpected windfall your site or property might enjoy, the use of the context of your immediate environment is relevant for your planning application, and clearly identifying your terms of reference will be helpful in that regard also.

For planning purposes, being able to explain the terms of reference for a building's architecture and the design thinking with the reasoning that lies behind the final design solution is often asked for by planning departments in the form of a design and access statement (see Book Four).

Whilst a simple domestic extension may not necessitate a D&A statement, there are many planning submissions that do, depending upon their level of planning complexity. However, even for a simple domestic project, whether it is a new building or a single-storey extension, a simple supporting statement setting out the existing design criteria, your terms of reference in relation to context, and the reasoning behind your design decisions is always welcomed by your local planning authority. It helps to make your planning submission more robust when referenced to context, and stating your reasoning behind your design decisions is always more convincing. It helps to make a more robust case for your planning appeal purposes should you find the need to go in that direction.

I refer further to the design and access statement in Book Four of this pre-planning book series when I deal more specifically with what planning documents are required when submitting your planning application.

Context, then, is referencing the design principles and values applied to the initial concept design for your building from what already exists. Assuming, of course, that the existing context is deemed to

A new recreation centre adjoining Metropolitan Open Land is surrounded by residential properties.
The Design and Access Statement demonstrated the attributes of the the building's design and its context which was imperative for the Planners' and Urban Designers' approval.
(Courtesy of Architect Knowhow Practice)

be of architectural value, but that is a different topic entirely not covered here, as we are currently focusing primarily on what needs to be actioned for your planning submission.

Whilst I referred to some typical examples of context earlier, context does not mean you have to slavishly follow what already exist. Of course not! However, being able to provide an architectural reference for your new modern building, perhaps even with unique design features in some way, is an important part of the architectural design process. In other words, the concept design development for your new building or extension for a specific site in a given location within a particular environment, etc. demonstrates inclusion and/or recognition of what already exists, and your final design solution should be reflected accordingly.

I should reinforce that being able to explain this design process by illustrating how your new building references its context is a prerequisite to attracting the planner's interest and serious attention. This will include demonstrating how particular attributes of the site have been incorporated into the architectural design. It will also show how your architectural design solution will negate the impact of any constraints, at best, or mitigate against the same in a meaningful way.

In Book Four, I make specific reference to preparing a design and access statement and highlight the importance attached to the same. For now, I will briefly mention I would usually use opportunities to demonstrate the depth of design thinking to the local planning authority when I prepare my design and access statement

for my planning submission. It is incumbent upon you or your architect (agent) to produce a planning submission where the design proposal is shown to be a worthy piece of architectural design work validated by a carefully prepared design and access statement. Certainly, this approach adds significant weight and kudos to your planning submission.

I know from personal experience that preparing a well-considered design and access statement where the story surrounding the concept design development is fully explained and referenced is what urban designers look for when commenting on planning submissions for the planning authority. Not every site, property, or planning proposal will attract the interest of the authority's urban designer, such as a simple rear extension, but gaining the interest of adjoining property owners is more usual. Where urban designers are commissioned to comment on projects for the local planning authority, they tend to be involved in projects which are contentious and at a level where the local planning authority will seek this additional assurance, advice, and guidance from a specialist consultant such as themselves. Being able to present a compelling case to validate your proposed design solution to the urban designer and win their support can have a meaningful impact, especially if that army of objectors appears on the horizon or are already banging on the door, as they are wont to do.

At this stage I have identified what context might mean, what relevance it might have for your new building or extension, and how that all makes up the built environment within which your site or property belongs. I am not suggesting you should be able to discuss and debate high-falutin theories in architecture, as that is not what is required. I would like to believe, however, that you have begun to think about your property and its context within the built environment in the simplest of ways. Developing a general awareness of what introducing a new three-dimensional element into your existing built environment might mean would be a good start, and one your local planning authority will appreciate.

In essence, your new three-dimensional building will interact in term of context on two levels, namely visually and functionally, and I will refer to this aspect again later when I discuss attributes and constraints.

A simple rear single-storey extension, however, is not the same as a four- or five-storey apartment block, a ten-storey office, or a massive distribution centre development. More especially, you should now have some basic appreciation and awareness as to how your new building or extension might change or influence the way the existing place will work in the future - not just for you as the building owner but also for the adjoining owners who have a similar stake in what happens around them. Your design proposal, therefore, needs to be alert to this fact and demonstrate the additional benefit and enhancement your design solution brings not only to the built environment but also to the community. Mainly in relation to single domestic development, you should seek to achieve a design solution where your proposal does not have any material impact on surrounding properties, in particular any adjoining properties.

A secondary school in South London designed to facilitate teaching and learning. (Courtesy of Architect Knowhow Practice)

Architectural Character

In the process of formulating my architect's appointment with my client for a particular project, I was informed they previously received a refusal for an earlier planning submission. Naturally I would need to know more, namely the reason for the refusal, as part of understanding the planning history of the property. Whilst I might not be surprised by the reason for refusal, more often than not the client would be flummoxed. Their failure to understand the planning refusal was not due to their lack of comprehension, per se, but was attributed more to the convenient standardised set of refusal reasons/options that appear to be discharged to expedite the planning delivery process (Gaine, 2021).

I often come across decision notices where the planning authority have issued a refusal because the proposed design for a new building or extension was deemed to be 'out of character with the area' - one of those convenient reasons.

Such decision notices tend not to provide any useful explanation as to why the design proposal is out of character. Neither is any reference cited to justify the planning refusal for the reason stated, apart from a few ubiquitous planning policies to substantiate the decision. Of course, planning case officers will cite every planning policy in their armoury to justify the planning refusal when they are of mind to but will never provide a detailed account as to why the design proposal is out of character.

Local authority planners might state it is not incumbent upon them to get the proposal correct and say that is the job of the agent, and in that they are correct. Moreover, local authority planners will always suggest availing of the pre-application advice process where they do offer planning advice, and in that, they are correct also.

When it comes to citing the character of an area, do they mean your design proposal is out of character because of its intended use, or is your proposal out of character because it appears not to reflect the visual attributes or the physical

The Guggenheim Museum Bilbao designed for the specific purpose of displaying art. (Image by Peggy and Marco Lachmann-Anke)

characteristics of the surrounding built environment generally? Or are they seeking to achieve something specific and unique, perhaps, for your site but are unable to communicate precisely what it is they expect?

Many believe the reason for this is that planning officials are not equipped to provide a detailed architectural response, primarily because they are not trained as architects who are experienced in delivering specific architectural design solutions for buildings and developments on a number of micro levels all at once. I would determine these micro levels by the building's functionality, by its association and influence of history and culture, by its intended use and its personality.

Architects, therefore, will consider a design solution for a building in terms of its functional character and the way the building is required to be used and designed accordingly. Thus, the manner in which a museum building is designed is very different to that of a school, an apartment block, or a hotel tower. A school has completely different requirements in order to function correctly than a museum. A museum building will have, for instance, a different requirement for daylight in order for that building to function correctly, as opposed to a school where the internal space arrangement will naturally be dictated by its function, where teaching and learning is the primary objective.

The character of buildings is sometimes referred to by the history and culture of the place which is often represented by the buildings' makeup and that particular built environment, and certain parts might be many hundreds of years old. For instance, whilst a spire would indicate a church as a gopuram depicts a Hindu temple, the cultural aspects highlight the associated character of those particular buildings. That is, we recognise and connect specific features of buildings, and we tend to associate these features with a particular architectural style and period of time, such as an Art Deco apartment building or a single-storey suburban bungalow.

Buildings, then, display character by their personality and in some ways are not too dissimilar to that of a human individual. Where a building is designed with a measure of integrity and honesty, it will demonstrate personal characteristics such as elegance, composure, and a measure of enthusiasm for what that building is meant to represent. In short, the building will have spirit.

Planning is a different discipline to architecture with a focus on master planning for towns and cities, managing land resources, and deciding on policy strategy. It controls new development and proposed changes to the existing built environment on a macro level. It determines future community needs in relation to housing, commercial, institutional, and industrial requirements.

As planning sets out a single overarching principle for an authority's development plan for a neighbourhood (neighbourhood plans and local plans), it does so as a general principle for the betterment of the general community and not in terms of detailed architectural design input for each building or development. In essence, planning is practiced in isolation of any architectural design expertise, as this is the domain of qualified architects, but planners will seek to impose their own architectural design preferences when it comes to assessing a planning submission and the detail design of the building.

At my pre-planning meetings with the planning case officer, I tend to ask them to explain why they might wish to change or adjust a particular architectural detail or feature. I do this with a measure of confidence because I have already tested and established in my own mind the design principles and features I have employed and can explain them ad infinitum. Given the planning system is discretionary, there is no requirement for the planning case officer to set out and explain their decision in architectural design terms. It is usually left to the applicant to consider an appeal, wherein the planning inspector will consider if the refusal is justified.

A planning appeal may be an opportunity for the applicant/architect to set out reasons why the proposed building design would not be out of character with the area, citing the usual design reasons along with appropriate terms of design references. The object of the exercise here, however, is not to entertain an appeal situation prematurely but to achieve a planning permission in the first instance. Consequently, it is just as well for the 'character' of the area to be examined and understood at the pre-planning stage and for the same to be demonstrated convincingly in the final design solution for pre-application purposes and the planning submission ultimately.

Classical Georgian houses in a streetscape .
(Image by bluebudgie)

In planning terms, architectural character can be described in a number of different ways, and sometimes it can have different meaning for different people without defining the specifics of the place. Character is sometimes referred to as being an element of architectural context, which applies more when we stand at a distance so as to examine a building in its overall setting. This means examining the building externally as an overarching architectural statement, an entity with mass and form against adjoining and surrounding structures, but without exploring the detail features of the building. In other words, we want to understand the physical and natural factors of the building to which the overall context relates, such as its location, its juxtaposition to other buildings and landscapes, its proximity to a nearby river or a nearby tower of some description, or a flyover cutting through a space, for example

Architectural character is often referred to as 'architectural style', and there is some measure of validity in this. However, architectural style depicts the period of architecture when it was built where aspects of the structure or a building in a streetscape are expressed by such characteristics as its culture and the meaning it gives the place.

I refer to this idea of architectural character as a building or a collection of buildings, as in a row, a street, or a cluster of buildings, which creates or sets a 'mood' for the place. We as individuals personally connect and relate with a given place, albeit at different levels, perhaps, and for different reasons. This will very often be influenced by our cultural background or our own individual terms of reference at a given time as well as our wider understanding and comprehension of the built environment that surrounds us as we comprehend it. That is, we automatically relate to the place as if we have a personal connection to it on an individual basis, for better or worse.

As architects and creators of the built environment at the micro level, our attention will naturally focus on design detail considerations such as the functional aspects and personal character of a building as well as the building's architectural composition and how that is expressed aesthetically. Architectural design operates where specific levels of thinking are employed which demand specific outcomes for specific buildings' users.

The image above (page 82), is a prime example of a Georgian building where the windows are clearly distinctive and representative of that period. We seem to have an innate grasp of the Georgian style and what a street consisting of Geor-

New house housing development adopting similar glass sub-division arrangement synonymous with the Georgian period.   (Image by James Feaver)

gian houses looks like. These windows, then, contribute to the character of the place by their size and proportions. They are synonymous with the overall proportions of the Georgian street as they were originally intended.

Consequently, using this example, the planning question to ask therefore is this: Would employing a Georgian-style window in a modern type of house be sufficient on its own to represent the true architectural character of a Georgian period street, house, or building? I suspect not, as it would take much more than a window with just a subdivision of glass panes to reflect the features and architectural meaning of a real Georgian street or house, where spaces and proportions both internally and externally are so different from what is the norm for domestic architecture today. Architectural design is more holistic than employing a window feature and expecting it to pass as a design solution for planning permission purposes. The site analysis will inform the architect about the existing character of the place, but that is only one facet of the architectural design process.

New house style in harmony with its natural environment.
(Image by giovanni gargiulo)

Architectural Style

Let us assume you have an opportunity to acquire a site in your dream location and want to build the house of your dreams. Let us also assume there are a number of other people interested in the same site who also want to build their dream house. I have every reason to believe your dream house will be different in many ways from other dreamers, even on the same site location. The moral of the story here is there is no one predetermined architectural style which could be defined categorically as the one and only correct design solution, because there simply is none. If there was, the local authority planners and urban designers would already have it designed and in detail, for certain, as part of their neighbourhood plan, and then where would we be? The planner's idea of utopia, I suspect, where architects cease to exist.

To properly highlight architectural style, go back in time a bit. For buildings and structures which relate to ancient Roman or Greek architecture, we all have an image in our heads as to what they represent and how they might be defined. They would ignite scenes of great structures and features depicting an architectural style. Structures and buildings constructed with great columns and their ornate capitals supporting great structures and often defining large spaces. The subtleties and difference in styles that exist between ancient Greek and Roman is not what I want to focus on here; I seek merely to alert you to the existence of a design style which prevailed in those ancient times and to highlight those different architectural features and architectural styles as a representation for that time.

Not all of ancient Rome and Greece consisted of such status symbols and structures which are a must-see when we visit these locations. Domestic architecture also prevailed in Rome. Some more delightful and grand than others, perhaps, with examples of the Roman villa against that of a streetscape almost akin to what we might identify today as an urban or suburban streetscape or street scene when compared to a detached property on an acre of land in a leafy location. Greece, too, had a population to house, and housing was a prerequisite for normal life there also.

If I move your thinking forward a number of centuries, let's bypass design styles like medieval, Renaissance, baroque, rococo, and Palladian architecture to arrive at architectural design styles like Georgian that I referred to earlier when discussing character. We perhaps also know about the Victorian style and what it represents and are familiar with the forty-five-degree angle bay window of that period as, indeed, the square bay of the Edwardian period. We conjure up images of all these styles, which are for many instantly familiar and recognisable.

We know what they look like in terms of the features they have, their shapes, their sizes, the arrangement of buildings, their proportions and roof formation, etc. We might have a greater affinity with these periods of architectural styles, as many people continue to live in such properties in different parts of the world. Because of this, we tend to know more about what Georgian, Victorian, Edwardian, or Art Deco styles look like because there are many examples of these styles of architecture remaining, within the British Isles and beyond.

I could continue with this topic and discuss and argue the niceties, likes, and dislikes of each and reference other viewpoints to support my take surrounding architectural character and style. However, what is more helpful for your purposes in pre-planning would be for you to gain a simple appreciation of architectural style for what it is you are dealing with when contemplating your new building project. I would hope, too, that you would acquire information which is sufficient for you to clarify your own thoughts and preferences connected with your new building or extension. I would also wish for you to identify and recognise your design reference for your site or property in particular and of course your

terms of reference to the built environment where you intend to add to or change it in some way.

Character and style, then, reference what your new building or extension has to live beside or fit in with some measure of harmony without disrespecting the character and status of the surrounding buildings where their presence does indeed have status. Your new building might refer to a period or style of architecture when a building or extension was built however long ago, assuming that the building in question has any architectural merit to justify recognition. Consequently, a new building might adopt or refer to a style of a different period, maybe because the owner or their architect likes particular aspects or features of that style or can justify that design approach architecturally, which can be equally valid.

New house addition respecting the existing by retaining existing roof geometry, window proportions and materials selection.   (Image by Author)

Notwithstanding the above possibilities, options, and choices, there is a planning requirement for the new building to justify its place as a physical entity which may suggest reflecting what already exists in terms of style so as to retain the architectural character of the place. However, this does not mean slavishly replicating the existing style in every detail. Architecture is more than that, and in the hands of a qualified architect a new, original interpretation of what already exists is what allows architectural design and style to evolve and remain current in terms of culture, relevant in terms of technology, appropriate in terms of its functionality, and exciting in terms of serving your vision or that or your client, naturally.

About Your Property

Perhaps I have prompted you sufficiently now to consider your own property in terms of its built environment context, character, and style in a simple, less convoluted architectural sense. You now need to have a look at these elements in relation to your own property, whether it is a parcel of land or an existing building on a parcel of land that you would like to demolish, rebuild, or extend.

Examine your property in relation to the surrounding properties. In other words, look at your property in context with what is happening around it. This means seeing how your property relates to adjoining properties on either side or the surrounding properties generally. I want you to get a feel for how your property currently 'fits

in' physically and visually within the existing architectural context, both as a footprint on the ground and as a physical entity occupying space in the air. After all, that is what buildings do!

By adding your new extension, roof conversion, or totally new building or development to what already exists, examine what that means in terms of introducing a physical change to the existing structure. Really examine if a bland box stuck on the rear or side of your property is a good solution visually. Or consider if there is an alternative to plonking a triangular blob on the roof will enhance the aesthetics of your property and surrounding properties.

The question you might wish to ask yourself, therefore, is this: Will what you are considering have a detrimental change by causing a material impact to the existing environment, or are you continuing the existing environment? Is your addition enhancing the place? Enhancement is always preferable. I would ask you to bear in mind that adding something additional can act as a vehicle for generating enhancement even just in a visual sense. Indeed, adding to an environment is not necessarily a bad thing from the start, as is often perceived to be by the objection lobby.

Your local planning authority will always be amenable to enhancement where architectural design is employed. They will be less enthusiastic or impressed, of course, about something that is just stuck onto your property like an incongruous lump or an ugly wart, or even plonked onto your site like a blob without any meaning or reference to the site itself or what already exists. Planners rightly complain about the volume of ill-considered and poorly prepared applications they receive. It is no wonder they find it easy to refuse certain planning permissions with the standard reasons as a matter of course (Gaine, 2021).

Examine, too, how your new building or extension contributes to the existing character of its immediate and wider surroundings, as discussed earlier. So consider for a moment what your intended new extension or new building might mean to the existing character of the area and what it will provide in terms of enhancement. Just because your proposed new extension or dormer roof construction is located at the rear of your property does not mean you are exempt from your design responsibilities - except, of course, if you believe anything will do because it comes under permitted development rights. Even that approach should be verified with a Certificate of Lawfulness if you want to decrease the risk associated with your development, as indeed you should.

Something just added merely to create internal space as the primary objective and in isolation of its external surroundings - its architectural context - is usually deemed to be a failure. Proposals of this calibre are usually described as out of character by the planners when describing the reasons for refusal. Suggesting some change with no regard to the surrounding buildings' form, the buildings' parts, the character of your property, or the character of the adjoining properties tends to not be viewed with much enthusiasm by the planning authorities.

Breaking the rhythm, character, and harmony of a streetcape should be subject to architectural design or planning control as opposed to depending on Design decisions made under permitted development. (Diagram by Author)

Architectural design and planning control in evidence when both have a common objective (Diagram by Author)

Projects of this nature tend to demonstrate investment purposes only, perhaps, or are a mere building exercise with the sole purpose of flipping (selling) the property. They tend also to be projects in total isolation to any architectural design merit, thinking, or context, as these factors do not normally form part of the overall project costs. In other words, your proposed design should demonstrate a reference to the site or property itself and what already exists in terms of specific architectural features, its attributes, and its constraints, thereby recognising the character as well as the challenges the surrounding built environment presents and showing it is designed accordingly. Finally, on this particular point, it is a known fact that where architectural design thinking, reasoning, and referencing are employed in the final design solution, the resale value is reflected accordingly as a matter of course. Approaching your project with a measure of awareness for arriving at an appropriate design solution, therefore, will prove itself to be a wise and prudent investment.

In the light of all that I have highlighted and described in terms of the built environment, architectural context, and of course architectural style, I would like to develop some focus as to what your particular property might consist of - what sort of factors and features relate to your property and how might they influence the concept design development for your new building or extension when it comes to preparing a planning submission.

Naturally, your building will have a building height, size and massing, a roof formation, hedges, trees, planting, proximity to boundaries, etc. Your building will have these features and factors, as will your adjoining and surrounding properties. They will contribute to how your new building or extension should be designed

and lend influence as to whether your proposed design represents a successful design solution or not.

Because every building occupies a space on the ground by its building footprint and space in the air by its volumetric mass, each building or group of buildings has presence and gives meaning to the place by the character and personality they exude, irrespective of whether you like it or not.

It is worth bearing in mind that all of these evolutionary planning processes in the UK and many other countries also go through a planning process to make sure the context of the place is not lost and there is a sense of continuity, harmony, and relevance. We would always hope that nothing is abruptly introduced to the built environment which would drastically interrupt its context and disturb the meaning of the place where meaning and continuity of context has value.

A building out of scale or too high or even lower than the adjacent structures interrupts the natural rhythm of the streetscape. This would be problematic visually and would naturally warrant some level of planning control. That is something out of keeping with what already exists. For instance, a proposal for a new single-storey building as an infill site within a street where three-storey buildings exist would clearly disturb the rhythm of that streetscape, see diagram page 87. It would look like a missing tooth. It could also be a piece of sculpture or even a new bridge that is out of context and disturbs the harmony with what is going on around it by its scale or massing. Introducing such a

The Guggenheim Museum building in New York page 89 (Image by Kai Pilger)

The Cloud Gate structure in Chicago (Photo by Max Harlynking)

Both occupy a public space within the built environment, and both allow human interaction in different ways.

physical entity, therefore, might be seen as disturbing the balance and order of the place by invading that space and having no regard to the visual impact generated as a result. This can apply to small domestic scale places and spaces as well as larger urban environments.

Of course, whether a bridge for functional purposes or a piece of sculpture for visual appreciation is designed and installed to promote 'art' as being the objective, there will be some of us who either love it or loathe it. Obviously, this is acceptable, whatever it might be, provided we understand and can explain why we love it or loathe it. Whatever the combination or mix of buildings, structures, spaces, art objects, bridges, or other artefacts that exist, they all have context in an architectural sense as structures do within spaces. They all make up the built environment where the character of the place has an established context and harmony and continues to evolve as such, which is referenced in turn by its buildings, structures, and spaces.

The characteristics of your building and every other building within your built environment will occupy a space as a three-dimensional volumetric entity. Perhaps not as grandiose a presence as the Guggenheim in New York or Bilbao (see page 79 and 88) but one which nonetheless has an identity and a personality in much the same way as the structures referred to here.

The original identity and personality of a place and its buildings continue to evolve by way of change and adjustment to the buildings' fabric. In many ways, they are also influenced by their owners' requirements and references. Your existing building and all the adjoining and surrounding buildings may be the same as your building, or they may not. Some may be the same and many may be different in some way from their original status when first built.

Your local planning authority will be privy to this evolutionary process by default. When it comes to making some changes by way of a new building or an extension, the discretion of the local planning authority comes into play along with the assistance of consultees and interested parties. This applies to not only domestic residential properties but also nonresidential properties such as a factory premises or office development.

Chapter Six

Attributes and Constraints

Overview

When I confirm my appointment with a client for a project, one of the first items on my agenda is to visit the site so I can assess what it has to offer. I approach this by examining the site itself in terms of the physical entities that exist within the site but I also examine what else exists beyond the actual boundaries of the site which may or may not impact the potential development of the site. In other words, I am interested to establish the physical entities that might have an influence in the design solution (see Book Two: 'Site Survey, Site Analysis, and Concept Development').

I always seek to incorporate any site attributes that may exist into the concept design development, and I highlight the features that have the potential to add value to the final design solution. At the same time, with any site constraints that exist, I will seek to manage these differently by designing them out as a first priority or designing a solution which mitigates against them as much as possible and to a point where it makes economic sense to do so. Sometimes a particular constraint or set of constraints are so impactful by their negative influence on the intended devel-

opment project they bring into question the actual viability of the project, where the financial return envisaged cannot be easily realised or there is a significant risk attached to the enterprise from the very beginning.

I refer to these types of features as attributes and constraints, as they can either assist or impede your design solution. Whilst attributes might allow you to capitalise on their presence, constraints, on the other hand, can become problematic in terms of satisfying a planning issue for others to employ as a weapon and can become a cost item for the construction process. In this chapter, I want to highlight and introduce to you how attributes and constraints can influence on your project (see Book Three: 'Attributes and Constraints').

You have often heard mention of 'pros and cons' or 'dos and don'ts', but this terminology does not really transfer well to an architectural design sense in a meaningful way. So when I identify the features and factors which make up a site or a property consisting of land and building(s), I refer to the site factors, features, and characteristics as attributes and constraints.

Attributes are positive features which can be worked with by the architect in a positive way, as they help to create additional added value to the final design solution and the client's potential for additional added value.

Conversely, constraints are the opposite in that they require the architect to minimise their impact on the development of the site and the overall project. Even better, where the architect can design out their impact entirely, this is always the better option and usually the most economical solution for the client also.

Attributes or constraints connected with your land or property can assist or impede the concept design development during the pre-planning stage, and they will influence how the architect's final design solution not only in relation to aspects of planning but also in relation to influencing the construction stage.

Attributes Definition

An attribute may be a feature of your land or building or both, as the case may be, which helps to facilitate your intended planning application. It might be an obvious valuable empty space or gap within your property, an obvious location for a new extension which does not impact any adjoining property because it might be totally or partially out of sight, let's say. The same set of circumstances might be seen as an opportunity for completing the architectural story to the building by filling the gap with additional building.

In other words, it truly lends itself to be built upon or filled in, and by doing so this adds additional space to the existing house or building in a most natural, obvious,

and sensible way. You might even say that space is crying out to be used for an extension, as it will enhance the original property or building in an unobtrusive and clear way. It will look like it was always meant to be part of the original property or building and not look like a stuck-on extension, per se.

Therefore, you have an opportunity to create additional space and at the same time create an architectural design solution which is in context and aesthetically correct, the whole of which makes for an excellent narrative for your design and access statement.

Another example of an attribute might be if you are intending to build a new building on a vacant site and locating your new building at a particular spot on the site that is clearly the most obvious and natural position for the new structure. This particular position works perfectly and in an obvious way because of the spectacular view it provides, let's say, which makes the best use of the site for the occupants in a very natural way.

You may be considering the actual purchase of the site specifically for this unique view in question. Moreover, what you have in mind is a good fit because it would not cause any material impact by the way adjoining properties are used by their owners.

Perhaps the adjoining properties already enjoy the same spectacular view and in a way similar to what you intend, which would suggest the local planning authority might have little, if anything, to be concerned about either. All of this would have to be verified, of course, by way of a planning submission. Notwithstanding the formalities of making a planning submission, they would be minded to grant a planning permission as a principle, but the actual building design (reserve matters) is another matter for the planners, as they usually tend to scrutinise the design details as part of their remit, as I referred to earlier.

In another situation, perhaps there is an opportunity to locate your intended building on a site which will not impact on any trees that might have a tree preservation order attached. This might suggest the visual impact of your finished building will provide real added value not only to your final design solution as a building for the specific parcel of land in question but also to the adjoining properties by the way your building will fit into the existing landscape, or streetscape, and complete the architectural story see image below.

Another scenario might be in relation to an urban or suburban environment. Perhaps your new building would add real value to the adjoining properties because it would actually fill in a gap in the streetscape which has existed for many years and is less attractive or visually exciting than it could be. It might even be an ugly eyesore. As an infill site about to be built upon, your design solution will enhance the overall appearance of the streetscape as opposed to the lot being left open and vacant or a dump for unwanted cars or a location for bonfires. In other words, your infill project will complete the architectural

A development opportunity where existing commercial use activities within a residential context could be changed to residential use with bulk and massing, see diagram page 87.   (Image by Author)

story for the street, and aesthetically it would fill that gap like a prosthetic tooth, thereby generating enhancement.

Equally, your infill development proposal will have a function of its own. In the example shown here, it will provide an opportunity for creating new apartment accommodations, which fits in with the neighbourhood plan's aspiration and requirements.

How the architectural design is managed for your infill site will be dictated by the strength of the character of the existing street and whether your architect can justify a radical alternative design to what already exists, which is possible too.

I had a project similar to this in that whilst not an infill site as such, it was a vacant corner site at the end of a street with architectural character of a historical nature. The local planning authority preferred to retain the openness of the place, as did that inevitable army of interested parties.

My client sought to achieve a design which reflected a more contemporary architectural style rather than follow the existing style. In fairness, the neighbourhood plan and design guides made it reasonably clear as to what would be deemed appropriate, and anything outside of that expectation was not acceptable for this area.

The client and I decided to prepare two design solutions: one depicting a modern architectural treatment and another elevational treatment to reflect the tradition feel of the street, which was Plan B. Given the site was on a corner, we felt we could refer to what was happening architecturally

on the other street with our preferred design solution, which was a mixture of architectural styles and not a repeat of the more historic reference. However, the case officer's report stated the land addressed the street with the strong architectural character and the style of the existing street with the historic reference. It had to be maintained as a prerequisite for that particular corner, as it would form a natural architectural conclusion to the street. The report did not present a very strong case for maintaining an open site and, indeed, that would have been somewhat difficult due to the fact that similar developments were happening elsewhere in this vicinity and there was no provision in the neighbourhood plan for this parcel of land to remain as open land.

The client, however, was wedded to his aspiration of a modern-style house and opted to make a planning submission on that basis. The planning strategy, then, was this: If the application was refused, he would take the next step with a planning appeal. In essence, the planning submission was made and refused, followed by an appeal. The appeal for the modern house design was refused also, but the inspector made a point of stating that a three-storey house on that corner was reasonable and thereby established the planning principle for the site to be developed, which was a huge win for the client. This meant that by the client presenting a design solution for a more traditional approach, it should be approved. I was able to pull our plan B out of the bag immediately, and within eight weeks the local planning authority issued planning permission without any fuss or shouting from objectors.

I have outlined some simple examples of what attributes might mean for your project, but in essence, any feature that can be capitalised on in terms of architectural merit for achieving a planning permission is deemed to be an attribute. As part of your pre-planning research and before you engage your architect, set about identifying what attributes are clearly obvious and worthwhile for you to investigate further as part of your own evaluation process.

Constraints Definition

Constraints, then, are the opposite of attributes. An example might be, let's say, the location of an adjoining owner's tree that is a prized possession and very dear to them. However, said tree will impede your construction process because where you would like to position your new building or extension conflicts with the roots. The root structure of that tree must not be interfered with, lest you cause damage to the tree. Designing out that problem can be a challenge and have a cost impact, I admit, but it is not insurmountable.

Other constraints that might impact or impede what you would like to do might be the geometry of your existing roof being so complex that interfering with it would be too costly for the new extension you are considering. In other words, the actual cost of connecting into the existing roof the way the local planning authority might insist on would prove to be so expensive that it might not warrant the cost of the new extension in the first place.

Similarly, there might be issues with the location of your existing drainage system, whereby the footprint of your new building will cover existing manholes, and those will have to be moved with their associated costs (see Book Three: 'Attributes and Constraints').

I have never had a project without some matter to be dealt with, managed, and, where possible, designed out as part of the final design solution. These factors are aspects you are better off identifying at the front end of the process so they can be included into the overall project costs before you commence with any building on-site. It behooves you to be alert to potential risk, as risk of any nature that is connected to a construction project means additional money has to be found to cover that risk.

Being faced with expensive project costs later can be a shattering experience and, in some cases, can bring the project to a swift end, leaving you with an incomplete building. I discuss attributes and constraints in far more detail in Book Three of this series and provide much more attention to the possible constraints you should be aware of. There are so many potential pitfalls and bear traps associated with constraints especially that I have created a separate book just focusing on these alone.

Attributes and constraints, therefore, will relate to your property in two distinct ways, influencing your project in both a visual capacity and a functional capacity.

Being aware of potential objections before they happen means you can mitigate against them at an appropriate time during your pre-planning process.   (Image by martinvickery)

Chapter Seven

Visual and Functional Interaction

Visual Impact and Influence

Now that you have an appreciation of how attributes and constraints might influence your design solution, I want to introduce you to how your project might be affected by these factors. In essence, this can happen in two distinct ways. There is a visual impact and influence or a practical and functional impact or influence, and sometimes even both.

In the first instance they relate visually to the type of property you have. That is, the building's form and shape, height, and massing will inform your new design as to what position, height, shape, and massing, etc. would be best for a new building when added to your existing building. Or even within a parcel of land (your site), if you are contemplating a new building, how appropriate is your design solution visually? In other words, what does your property look like now against what it will look like with a new building or new extension added (see Chapter 5: 'Context Appreciation')?

Let's examine visual impact for a moment. What would your view be if I owned a parcel of land next to your property and aspired to provide myself an economic place to live? Let us assume for the moment that the character of the site has merit and is worthy of reasonable recognition, if not protection.

I have decided to propose a standardised manufactured box solution. You know the type I mean - what you often see on a building site being used for temporary site offices. They are cabins, really, but some bright spark like me believes that by assembling a collection of these metal box cabins together and calling it a 'building' of some description, all will be well. Trust me - I am an architect!

You might suggest my intended container architecture proposal would not be appropriate. It is not a design specific for the features of the site or unique to the character of the site nor one that matches the character of the area generally. In other words, it is out of context visually with what is going on in and around the site. Bearing in mind that you are an adjoining owner, you already know both of our sites are unique because each site has its own unique features and characteristics, its own mood and feeling which results from what already exists within the site and its surroundings. Each site has to be treated as such with its own individual personality. So, you (and perhaps others) would maintain that me plonking down a standardised box cabin or a series of box cabins on the site without due regard for the existing architectural context is not architectural design.

However, it is worth indicating that as an architect, I could justify employing the architecture and engineering associated with container architecture and produce a design solution for a habitable space. My site does not need to be located within an urban context (more synonymous with container architecture, I would suggest), as I believe I could produce a visually attractive design solution and demonstrate strong reasons to validate such a design proposal. I could also present very strong architectural arguments and design reasons as to why my container architecture solution would be an appropriate architectural design solution for this site in question. I could support my planning submission further by citing aspects associated with technology advancement, carbon reduction, climate change reasons, and similar suchlike validation.

I am satisfied, too, that I could do a very good job in describing the attributes of the site and how I employed them in a most productive and sensible manner. I believe I could provide a full, convincing description of any constraints that might be raised by those seeking to undermine the validity of my design proposal. I would do all that as part of my design and access statement, and I would evidence the same in a robust fashion. I believe I

could feel very satisfied with myself and that my planning submission for a container architecture solution would indeed be a robust submission.

However, I cannot guarantee the local planning department would accept my proposal or the supporting evidence. Like you, they may wish to object for various reasons and employ various planning and design guides to reinforce and validate their discretionary decision for delivering their planning refusal, for which you now know they have a standard set of reasons to justify that refusal decision.

My architectural design prowess, therefore, good and great as I might believe it to be, really amounts to diddly-squat if the local planning authority have a different view, possibly supported by objectors, and elect to dispense their discretionary powers accordingly. This might be the case if my site is located within a context where adjoining properties consist of an assembly of period Georgian properties, for instance, or are too closely connected to any other sensitive structure, like a specific Listed Building.

If this were the case, as an architect I realistically might be expected to know more than just firing off my planning submission without carrying out some level of due diligence and, indeed, making a more informed design decision for my site. This would mean undertaking the necessary planning research and investigations first and taking advantage of the pre-application process just so I could eyeball the planning case officers across the table and measure the strength of their position against my own. I discuss this in more detail when I cover aspects associated with

My dream house can be with container architecture also! (Image by Hithesh S)

the pre-application process in Book Two and again in Book Four.

As I mentioned previously, I could have my more conventional design solution at the ready. That is my Plan B scheme, tucked away in my bag ready to pull out and discuss if I felt that was what I wanted to do at the time in the interest of being sensible and pragmatic and not on an ego trip, perhaps. Realistically, I suppose, that might depend on just how wedded I was to my container solution and if I needed a place to live.

I could ignore any advice obtained through the pre-application process indicating that a refusal is the likely outcome following any planning submission from me, but I proceed with my planning submission anyway just to achieve a planning decision. The planning decision will provide me with a set of reasons for the refusal which I can work with when preparing for a planning

appeal should I elect to go in that direction. A planning appeal might only be attractive to me if I am really totally committed to my container house solution for that particular site. The other alternative for me might be to accept the conventional design option, get a planning permission, sell it, collect the added value the planning permission will realise, and find a site location where I can build my dream container house, as I know it will be beautiful!

The architectural design for your new building or extension, therefore, will also relate to the visual context within which it is located and that which surrounds it. You might already do this subconsciously, but I would like you to really scrutinise what you see as your property, whether it is a parcel of land or a building (or both) and identify its architectural context. Really look and examine what features on the site really exist within your property, adjoining your property, and beyond it. Record your findings for your Research & Project Folder and as part of your planning submission later.

Start with adjoining buildings first or buildings located on the perimeter of your site boundary. Examine the building form, heights, and massing which surround or adjoin your site or property. As part of my concept development, I would draw a section through my site which would include the properties immediately beyond the site boundaries just so I could assess and evaluate the height and space relationships between the two.

Examine how these building(s) as a primary feature influence how your site and/or existing building works as it is, and then take on board any other features in relation to how your site works. This might be aspects relating to access, overhead cables, public service, and similar suchlike characteristics. In addition, I would expect you to refer to Chapter Five where aspects relating to context, character, and style are discussed which you should evaluate in relation to your site as a holistic enterprise.

You should also note the orientation of the sun and ensure you evaluate the impact of the sun throughout the year. As you will not be designing a building just for the day, you must assess the site and property as well.

In essence, by scrutinising your site you are in fact analysing the site for its attributes and constraints. You are assessing the surrounding built or natural environment of your property, depending on its location. Then, consider for a moment introducing a new ingredient, such as your new building or extension, and what the external feeling will be like for you as the building owner and for your adjoining owners also. These are core issues that have to be taken by the scruff of the neck and managed in a sensitive manner in order to achieve a successful design solution for the property location.

So what I have just highlighted, then, is the visual impact your new building or extension will have on your existing property, whether it is a parcel of land or an existing building. In fact, you are assessing the visual impact your proposal will have on the adjoining and surrounding properties, which will depend on their proximity to your property or building. Whatever you decide to put forward as a design solution, therefore, it will never be in isolation of what is happening around it on the ground and in the space above.

In other words, ask yourself: What if I select to do this or that as a design solution - will that be an appropriate architectural design response and a 'good fit' within the existing architectural context? How do I know that, and how can I explain my design solution as part of my planning submission? Additionally, how will my design proposal look and fit within the built environment of the neighbourhood or district, and how best can I explain that? Will it add value and enhancement to what already exists, and how does my design solution demonstrate that as well?

I want to mention here that I am aware and alert to the fact that in many cases where building and extensions relates to a domestic property with a focus on family living, most people just want to extend their property so as to generate additional family living space. You might well ask: What is all this highfalutin thinking and jargon for? Is it necessary and does it apply to my simple domestic extension? Well, yes, it does apply to your property and all properties where you consider the built environment relevant to your property.

I am also aware of the ability to undertake a simple build where permitted development rights apply. Indeed, the reason I seek to bring architectural awareness of your site/property and your immediate and the wider built environment to your attention is precisely to avoid the results the permitted development route option appears to generate much too often. The permitted development outcomes I am referring to are not just in relation to architectural design but other more serious difficulties homeowners sometimes find themselves in after following incorrect advice.

Building in Isolation

I would like to cite a further example of visual impact and for you to note the manner in which this building work is handled. I refer to it as building work because I fail to see much architectural design employed that is worth discussing.

The thrust of this project, see image below, lies with the removal of a pitched roof and then building over it with an additional floor level, providing a number of apartments above the ground floor level.

In my opinion this is a very sad building, primarily because what has been allowed to happen is a very poor architectural substitute for what already existed originally. In other words, there is no evidence of enhancement. This result is so divorced visually from the immediate context of the existing adjoining buildings and the space occupied by the much taller building opposite, it makes a mockery of the position it occupies, especially on

A recent building occupying a prominent corner location.   (Image by Author)

Less than impressive planning or architectural design solution for a prominent corner location. (Image by Author)

a corner in a prominent position. Isolationism prevails here.

I believe it to be out of context and character with what is happening around it, and because it fails to address the whole of this junction with any level of architectural design principles or meaning or sympathy, it is truly sinful.

I fail to see any reference to the scale or any sense of respecting the proportions of what is happening around it. Its massing, too, totally dominates its immediate neighbours, and it fails to harmonise visually with the adjoining buildings. It is like a lump of building plonked on top of and in between other buildings. And yes, you might ask, how did they obtain a planning permission for something which is clearly an exercise in building as opposed to being of architectural merit?

I really don't know the answer. My best response might be that I can only assume an urgency for housing accommodation prevailed at the time which overrode planning restrictions normally applied elsewhere in the borough.

Perhaps an emphasis should have been placed on acquiring the whole of the properties occupying this corner location as an overall planning strategy for this prominent location. Maybe they could have emphasised a grant planning permission with beneficial to be made obvious to the developer so as to make the entire enterprise more worthwhile, particularly when a number of buyouts would have been necessary.

The commercial entity at the ground floor could have been maintained very simply with an opportunity for a greater number of habitable units above, even with a taller building, which architecturally would make much greater sense as an architectural design solution in this particular corner location. Moreover, this particular corner location is directly opposite a major development site on the opposite corner already scheduled for significant urban regeneration, which one would reasonably believe would have been on the same planners' radar. Consequently, a real opportunity has been lost by not considering the overall strategic planning for this development site and location in conjunction with the major development site opposite in a holistic manner, thereby providing some level of meaning and identity to the place that the community could be proud of.

Moving on and away from this example, I would expect the visual context of your property in relation to the adjoining and surrounding properties is likely to be the primary feature in terms of reference for your local planning authority. It will be instrumental for their decision-making purposes, particularly in relation to the front and side elevations which is where you may be contemplating a new extension, let's say.

They will assess and evaluate your planning proposal against the adjoining and surrounding buildings and whether your proposal will or will not fit in as the planning case officer views it. If your site is located on a corner, also consider how your proposal might be influenced by the traffic movements at that road junction in terms of safety or if your proposal will interfere with sight lines. Of course, they will consider this and any observations they may receive from the interested parties I referred to previously.

They will seek to determine, then, whether they consider your planning proposal to be 'out of character' with the area, which is a term they use in their notice of refusal, or they will cite other reasons if they believe a planning refusal is an appropriate decision.

As part of their evaluation process, they will also take note of other types of physical features and factors if they exist. Features like a river, perhaps, adjoining your site or trees or a colony of bats known to be in residence on your property. Perhaps great-crested newts, the subject of much ire, are a protected species and occupy a pond on your site, or maybe your property is adjacent to a particular road with known traffic issues.

All of these physical factors and features and more besides can cause a functional impact on your design solution, which can then influence the decision of your local planning authority. Your local planning authority usually refer to their own planning guidance to assist them in making their planning decisions, as they did in the corner site highlighted below, see page 104.

When I researched the local planning files to understand the background to this planning permission, I was immediately attracted to two specific planning documents. The first was the support statement (a mini design and access statement) by the applicant and the second was the planning case officer's report. In reading and assessing the reasoning put forward by both, I could see the correlation between the two documents in that the primary substance of both were, for all intents and purposes, in unison. In the first instance, the references made by applicant to the planning policies were appropriate and pertinent to the specifics of the application site; it cited the London Plan and supporting planning policies to highlight how the design solution met those criteria. There was no highfalutin

Roof conversion and new additional house attached at side transforming an existing pair of semi-detached properties into terraced properties   (Image by Author)

language - just a very simply worded submission which was relevant and to the point, and the applicant's points were well made.

Equally, the planning case officer (PCO) in her report cited the same policy documents and set out the specific context and character attributed to the site and the surrounding built environment as she viewed it. The PCO's report also referred to the internal consultation responses (internal consultees) and the external notification responses (the adjoining property owners) where two objections were received. Presumably they came from the immediate adjoining properties, as they would have the greatest impact by this planning submission, particularly with regard to the proximity of adjoining boundaries and properties, which I personally felt was close. However, the planning authority assessed this and considered there to be no loss of natural daylight due to the orientation of the site and adjoining properties. Whilst a set of normal reasons of objection were presented to the local planning authority, their reasons were considered to be insufficient for a decision to refuse to be issued, whereby a grant of planning permission was the ultimate result.

In this case, the application made the task of the local planning authority reasonably easy and straightforward. The correct research and investigation was seen to be carried out, the findings incorporated into the final design solution. Additionally, the design solution was explained well enough in the supporting statement for the planners to appreciate the design thinking employed.

If you are already considering a new extension, you may now be thinking about how it might best connect into your existing property visually and if any constraints exist in your situation. I have given you some simple examples of constraints earlier, but for some projects they might also mean proximity to boundaries, complicated roof formation (which can be expensive), proximity of trees (especially if they are on the adjoining property and outside your control), and proximity of existing windows to an adjoining property (which prevents you building close, as there is possibly a 'right of light' matter, and this would generate a planning issue).

Practical and Functional Influence

The second way attributes and constraints relate to your property is when certain project specifics, physical entities, or features attached to your existing property. They may have a potential impact on the practicalities associated with achieving a planning permission in the first instance but also on the construction process which follows later. Additionally, attributes and constraints may affect the building's functionality in some way, and certain design consideration has to be employed to circumvent that situation. An example of this may relate to a restricted access, some overhead obstruction, or the location of a tree within an adjoining property which has a tree preservation order attached to it, thereby preventing any surgery to the tree, which can be an expensive inconvenience.

These may have a bearing on how your design solution is developed for construction purposes, and your planning solution is reflected accordingly. Construction op-

tions and possibilities tend to focus on the practicalities surrounding construction process and the options that exist, both for efficiency and for economic benefit, whilst functionality will focus on how best to use the building and its spaces both internally and externally.

Construction considerations tend not to have a direct influence or connection on a planning decision by your local planning authority because planners are usually more interested in how the new building or extension will fit in and appear within the character of the area. There are occasions where interested parties seek to weaponise the construction process as a means to influence a planning decision. How you get it built is not normally a concern the planners engage in. However, for your own due diligence and sanity, perhaps, make sure you are able to actually construct your building as stated on the planning application drawings and supporting planning documents.

I have encountered situations where the planning drawings, whilst suitable for the local planning authority's purposes, were in no way suitable for construction purposes. In fact, some cases put forward as suitable for planning application purposes were next to impossible to construct or, at best, not a sensible or logical construction solution. Clearly they were executed by somebody not concerned in how to build it but merely preoccupied in achieving a planning permission in isolation of the construction process that follows, because usually that was all that was asked of that person by the client.

Air brick to provide natural ventilation to existing ground floor timber structure and void below.
Damp proof course (DPC) below air brick which should be a minimum of 150mm above finished ground level
(Image by Author)

These are design considerations, then, which should be assessed up front at least minimally by an experienced agent in the pre-planning stage, as they can influence not only the direction a planning application might take but also how the building might be best constructed for practical purposes, speed, and cost efficiency. To this end, it is imperative certain design questions are asked at the pre-planning stage, and such questions are usually raised in relation to building control matters. This is not to suggest a building control application needs to be prepared in parallel with a planning submission; that is not the case. However, it is wise and prudent for building control matters to be examined at the outset, at least, lest a costly element will present itself during the construction stage.

In developing some initial design proposals for your planning submission, features like drains might impact matters if they are in an awkward location and might need to be adjusted or relocated. Existing external pipes might have to be ducted internally through your new extension or rerouted.

Ground levels might have to be adjusted to accommodate your existing internal floor levels, but a difference in floor levels might lend itself to creating a split-level internal space, which can enhance how the overall spaces work together but might attract a cost.

Solving a difference in ground levels might cost money that you would prefer not to have to accommodate as a matter of course, but I have seen cases where this has not been taken into consideration. Thus, the existing suspended timber floors were left in a decaying condition

Telescopic ventilators incorporated into new external cavity wall construction to ventilate the void space below the new beam and block ground floor structure. (Image by Author)

due to no cross ventilation. Making sure existing air vents to the current ground floor voids are not covered over is something a trained architect will ensure as a matter of course. I have seen cases however, where this has not been taken into consideration and the existing suspended timber floors are left to decay due to the cross ventilation being cancelled by not incorporating an air duct from the existing floor void out to the perimeter wall of the new extension.

It might be that a manhole cover is in the wrong place and needs to be relocated, but this issue needs to be designed out. Otherwise, your planning drawings are meaningless for construction purposes, and this is where building control approval becomes an important issue. You might even need to contact your local water authority during the pre-planning stage to satisfy yourself that the proposed building

footprint will not impact any below-ground drains belonging to that water authority, as they may not approve you building over certain elements of their drain. This might necessitate a redesign or accepting to reroute their drain, which can be a project cost you may not have expected. Consequently, your research and investigations are vital so as to not fall into the trap of securing a planning permission in isolation of these physical factors, rendering your planning permission virtually useless for construction purposes.

It might be an issue of access to your property where delivery vehicles cannot drop off materials and supplies close enough to the actual location of the work. This might create additional manhandling, which will be inconvenient for the builder but who will include an additional cost for this extra manhandling of goods when they are tendering for your project.

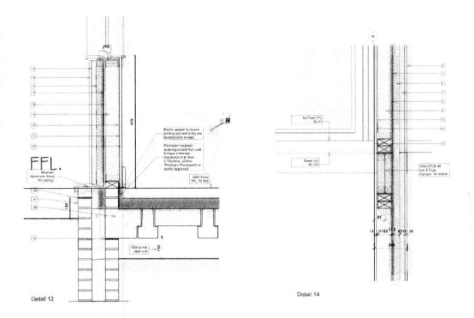

Typical construction drawing information enabling the builder to price accurately
and build correctly   (Courtesy of Architect Knowhow Practice)

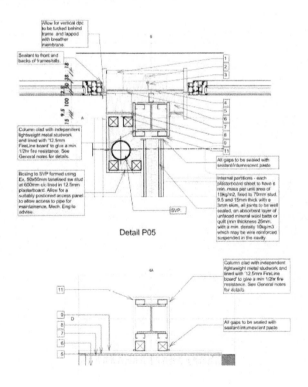

Detail P05

It might be a situation that your property is a two-storey terraced property and the only way of getting your new rear addition built is by allowing your builder and his crew to traipse through the whole of the ground floor area for a few months which might be acceptable if you are not living there. But for many homeowners this is not always possible.

Project viability can be influenced by the ease with which your site can be accessed (Hogan-O'Neill, 2021). However, you might already be alert to a viable option available through a prefabricated modular architecture solution. There are occasions when some sideways thinking can make a project work. Perhaps a totally factory-assembled and fitted-out modular building could be delivered from a factory on the back of a delivery truck lifted over your roof and into position at the rear. This can be a very viable option, and one which can be installed and completed on-site within a week with the minimum of disturbance and foundation work required. This is a different procurement process from the conventional on-site construction process. It is more specialised insofar as the design and manufacture of the building requires a different type of architectural design skills and management expertise.

A Brief Insight into the Modular Option

Modular buildings and modular homes have always appeared to be synonymous with one another, although there are also examples of modular buildings that are factory produced for other sectors too. The term 'modular' has a long association with prefabrication and system buildings where aspects of factory built, mass-production and standardisation highlight some of the typical characteristics that remain omnipresent in the minds of many.

There is a clear distinction between that described as on-site activities associated with conventional 'modular building' or 'modular construction' which is an- on-site construction process as opposed to a premanufactured 'modular building',

A pre-manufactured modular unit under assembly within a factory and fitted out internally prior to delivery to the site location.   (Courtesy of Structural Timber Projects Ltd.)

A pre-manufactured modular unit forming a rear extension solution delivered from the factory and lifted over and into position at the rear of the house. (Courtesy of Structural Timber Projects Ltd.)

which is an end product derived from an assembly process from within a factory.

The only element of the building's superstructure that has any relationship with the actual site, therefore, is at the time when the modular units are assembled together at the site to form the complete modular assemblage. Indeed, this final assembly process does not require skills normally associated with conventional construction as the complete building's assemblage is carried out by the manufacturer and not the contractor.

The common denominator that might continue to validate any relationship of 'modular building' or 'construction' as an on-site process is the interface between factory and site and, this is to a very limited extent in the context of modular buildings. The interface is the activity that takes place between the manufacturing process and the completed modular assemblage at the site location. It constitutes a measure of on-site work referred to as 'enabling works' for the modular units to be assembled into a modular superstructure.

Many modular buildings are commissioned as self-supporting single storey buildings or, even two and perhaps three or four storeys high in some instances are not uncommon. The nature and extent of the interface in this instance is limited whereby the enabling work required above ground for the modular superstructure is minimal and limited to the top of the foundations or, the installation of a concrete slab upon which the modular units are to be fixed. The interface then, is the connection between the factory assembly process and any on-site enabling work required for the purpose of completing the modular assemblage at the site location.

Modular buildings are now becoming taller and depending on the height of the modular building being proposed the central core areas might be constructed as a reinforced concrete structure. Buildings procured in this way are no different in terms of satisfying planning and building control requirements as the same rules and regulations apply.

In essence, prefabricated and modular architecture is identified as being two specific entities. In the first instance modular buildings can be delivered though panelisation whereby specifically designed walls, roof, and floor panels are manufactured within a factory environment and delivered to the work site for assembly into the pre-designed building. This is a precision design process where each panel has a specific location within a wall or floor or roof. Panelisation is deemed to be more connected with the conventional construction process primarily because of the actual nature of the on-site assembly process.

Modularisation on the other hand is a totally premanufactured process where the three dimensional volumetric unit is often referred to as volumetric modular. Modular units can vary number and be of different shapes and sizes for a building. They are manufactured and fitted out internally within the factory environment allowing completed volumetric modules to the delivered to the site for their final assembly together as a complete assemblage.

The plan form of a modular building is however defined more by the size of the modular units or modules which, when assembled together result in a finished assemblage referred to as the modular building. Whilst modular houses, apartments and extension are usually rectangular in plan shape; for non-residential buildings however, the size of the standard modular unit forming the total assemblage will dictate what can be accommodated within each module forming the internal spaces

On-site assembly process for two new apartment tower blocks in South London.   (Image by Author)

Modular unit guided into position for final assembly. (Image by Author)

and the core areas. Some modular buildings will necessitate a number of modular units in order to create a single space to accommodate all of the common activities required. Core areas are not necessarily located in the centre of the building and the location at each end of the building is a common practice so as to adhere to the building control and means of escape requirements.

The thrust behind the architectural design and production of premanufactured modular buildings in the UK continues to grow, albeit at a slow pace over the past two decades. Technology coupled with a measure of design ingenuity have together created a roadmap to take modular buildings to new heights, forty and more storeys high in some cases. High rise modular buildings are now possible where the structural integrity of the building is derived from the modular units themselves through the design and manufacturing process where the lower level modular units have the structural capacity to support the modular units above.

Within a high-rise modular building the thickness of the walls would naturally be thicker at the lower levels and reduce in thickness as the building increases in height thereby allowing some additional space to be created within the upper level modular units. This approach to designing high rise modular buildings eliminates the need for any secondary structural support such as steel framing and reduces a high degree of enabling work at the site.

Design options associated with modular buildings are currently enjoying a renaissance where perceptions previously held surrounding prefabricated and Modular Architecture (PAMA) are under serious review. It is already demonstrated that modular units can be assembled and totally fitted out internally within the factory environment and delivered for their final assembly at the site. Consequently, the notion of industrialised construction in the UK is rapidly becoming a realisation which brings premanufactured modular architecture into a clearer focus for providing architectural design solutions and a certain reality for architects to recognise. Total PAMA however, will not be achieved until the total completion of the external cladding treatment forms part of the factory manufacturing process which is not yet the situation to a satisfactory level of design and precision. The confidence attached to existing external cladding solutions does not exist to the point where a measure of perfection or acceptance is achieved to satisfy the aspirations of most architects. Further research and design development is necessary by architects in particular if this final challenge is to be accomplished.

There are occasions where certain physical features and characteristics connected with the site place a level of constraint with regard to employing conventional construction processes. However, by undertaking some fundamental assessments and analysis as to possible alternatives, prefabricated and modular solutions can overcome many of these, especially in relation to the provision of residential solutions.

Matters relating to satisfying architectural design and planning matters are not affected by employing a prefabricated or modular solutions and in some instances can bring significant advantages to both in terms of project delivery with a 'green' label.

Whilst attributes and constraints revolve around the practicalities of having your building constructed, they can also dictate how an architectural design solution can be developed for your intended planning submission purposes, irrespective of whether the project is delivered through conventional construction or prefabricated modular process. Identifying and managing their influence and potential impact allows more certainty in creating a more sensible, cost-effective construction at the concept design stage.

Having some appreciation of what attributes and constraints can mean at your pre-planning stage in terms of the practicalities connected with getting the construction process correct in parallel with preparing your planning submission is always worthwhile. It alerts the concept design process wherein constraints need to be designed out and attributes are capitalised to the fullest in the final design solution, which is ultimately presented to the local planning authority for their planning decision.

Book Three provides a much deeper insight into attributes and constraints, especially constraints which are discussed in much greater detail because of the serious impact they can have. Some of the more typical attributes and constraints issues that tend to come up in projects which you may not be aware of until you are presented with the situation with no advance warning are highlighted. There are a host of issues that are normally encountered on most projects and more besides.

Of course, you do not really think of all these issues and potential tricky bits and situations until you are faced with them, especially if you are a homeowner merely contemplating improving your home. I am hoping, however, that because you have worked your way through this first book in this pre-planning series you have a much better insight as to what is generally involved when it comes to managing the planning process either on your own behalf or that of your client. For those already engaged in the planning process in whatever area of professional activity, I hope a further level of enlightenment has been provided by this book.

Consequently, before you even consider making a planning submission, it is im-portant you make yourself aware of these possible events before they actually occur. As a self-manager/client or an agent acting on behalf of your client, your objective is to design out or mitigate these often nightmarish scenarios by undertaking your research and investigations at the front end of your project, for which Parts One, Two, and Three of this series will guide you through step by step.

Chapter Eight will provide you with a general overview of the planning process and some indication as to what you should expect when preparing a planning submission. It is not intended to provide you with a detailed account of what is required, but it is sufficient for you at this time when you simply need to know what is involved and what to watch out for.

Completed assemblage - two new modular
apartment buildings with external
cladding systems applied to
modular units as an on-site
installation Process.
(Image by Author)

Planning Permission or Permitted Development

Preparing a Planning Submission

Achieving a planning permission is not always out of reach or impossible to achieve. Indeed, planners will suggest a planning permission for your site or property is always achievable where the planning policies and design guides are adhered to in the first place. Moreover, they will highlight where they are prepared to make some measure of adjustment to your proposal where your proposal demonstrates some degree of merit for the site.

In essence, there has to be a very sound basis surrounding your planning submission because for the building/development project to be granted a planning permission, the intended use and functionality of the building/development must demonstrate appropriateness on a number of levels. Project proposals should also indicate a valid and viable business case is in place for the development project, which can be anything from a simple extension to a significant building or development.

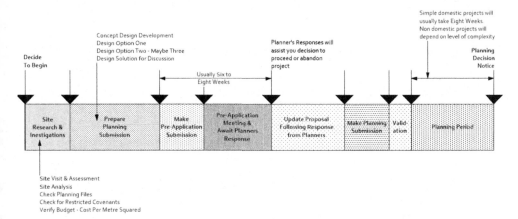

Planning Permission Route

(Diagram by Author)

What is often an issue, however, is that what you might aspire to create on your site or property does not altogether accord with the goals and expectations your local planning authority might envisage. They might, for instance, view your site as being able to provide more for the community than what your proposal has to offer. Conversely, perhaps your design proposal is seen as too ambitious for the site by indicating over development. In between the goals and aspirations of both camps there is always a design solution which can be agreed upon, but this might mean both you and the planning authority surrendering certain aspects in order to achieve a planning permission, and this is where your pre-planning preparation is all important.

It is always worth bearing in mind that when it comes to seeking a planning permission in the UK, the reality is that you are at the mercy of the planning system itself, primarily because it is a discretionary planning system. This means irrespective of what is stated in development plans or neighbourhood plans, your local planning authority has total discretion to grant or refuse you planning permission for a variety of reasons, and there can be plenty of them outside their official planning policies and design guides.

Such planning reasons can include political influence, adjoining owners' objections, interested party objections, and a host of other opportunists besides. Hence, a sense of paranoia and anxiety can evolve for many applicants, especially for homeowners wishing to add an addition or business owners seeking to enhance their premises to make their business op-

erations more functional, even with community interest at stake such as employment. The larger commercial developers, on the other hand, are more familiar with the planning process. Even though many have an army of consultants and specialists to take on the management and the headaches associated with the planning process for them, they too can become embroiled in the planning shenanigans.

Notwithstanding the jumps and hoops many applicants and their architects find themselves presented with along the way, it is a known fact that planning success has a better chance of being realised where a well-considered and properly prepared planning submission is recognised as a prerequisite from the beginning.

Follow the Process

In order to make a successful UK planning submission, you should recognise a process exists whereby you have to carry out certain actions for certain events at certain times as you progress through preparing your planning submission.

A skilled architect by default will be well acquainted with the various nuisances surrounding the planning processes and procedures. Architects are equipped to know where to begin and how to manage a project through the pre-planning and pre-application stages and finally completing the formal planning submission. For the layperson, however, with aspirations of self-managing a project, the same degree of competence would not be expected, but it is still important to recognise a process exists. Having at least a rudimentary understanding of how the planning process works is significant if you are to have any level of success.

Adhering to the process means self-discipline is required, as there is no point venturing off on a tangent just because you fancy it or because some particular aspect appeals to your sense of priorities. You will find your work efforts and time to be a good investment when you stick to the plan of work, keep focused, and complete the tasks in some semblance of order. The diagram 'Planning Permission Route' sets out the overall plan of work normally associated with most projects and obtaining a planning permission. This work and effort applies whether you are seeking to add value with a new development on a parcel of land or adding additional floor area to an existing building in the UK.

There are of course situations where development is permitted without having to submit a formal planning application, such as the UK's permitted development rights. The US has a similar facility referred to as an 'As-Of-Right' development which means a development which complies with all applicable zoning regulations and does not require any discretionary action by the City Planning Commission or Board of Standards and Appeals may proceed.

In the UK, permitted development rights has a perception which relates more to domestic residential development, but

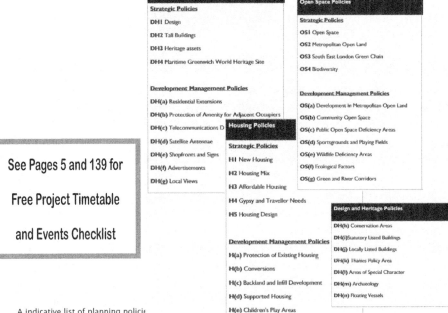

See Pages 5 and 139 for

Free Project Timetable

and Events Checklist

A indicative list of planning policie
your local planning authority may request additional
information to support of your planning submission.
(Courtesy of Royal Borough of Greenwich)

recent planning changes have opened up opportunities for commercial residential also (see Chapter 8: 'Permitted Development').

I want to bring your attention to some vital information you need to be aware of surrounding your property asset in the first instance but also what information is usually expected by your local planning authority when making your planning submission. The list shown opposite is an indication of the type of additional information, by way of additional reports, your local planning authority might ask for in relation to the specific policies they may apply to your site and its location. Each project and planning submission is always unique, as every site and location will be unique, which in turn requires a unique design solution.

Consequently, you will not normally be asked for everything listed here but only that which is deemed relevant for your planning submission. Such documents or special reports requested by your local planning authority will be dictated by the circumstance surrounding your planning submission. The best time for you to find out about what likely reports or supporting information will be required for your planning submission is when you instigate the pre-application advice process. Indeed, it would be incumbent on the applicant or the agent to request clarification at the pre-application meeting as to what supporting information the planning authority will require in order for the planning submission to be rendered complete so that validation can take place.

The nature and extent of the planning documents required for your submission, of which the planning drawings form a part, are dictated by the nature, size, and level of complexity attached to what you intend to build or seek as a change of use for a property. In addition to this, and due to any complexities or contentious issues that may arise, your development project might attract a requirement for other planning documents to be included in order to have your submission for planning validated.

Consequently, if you are a homeowner or a lay-person unfamiliar with how things work, I want you to recognise from the outset that there are some very important steps you need to know about and follow before you rush off getting things done which are possibly out of sequence with the correct process. Do not have drawings prepared or jump in headfirst submitting your planning drawings and an application form or having a chat with a friendly builder, which, incidentally, is definitely not what you should do at the start of your project. At this initial pre-planning stage, even you do not have a total grasp of what the issues might be for your project, so discussing your development project with anybody is premature and not recommended.

Neither should you even be tempted to discuss your intentions with owners or occupiers of any adjoining properties. Indeed, I would strongly suggest you refrain from any such notions, because at the initial stages of any project you do not know the viability of your project in terms of permission, let alone obtaining advice or price guidance from a builder. At this initial stage, you are merely thinking about your development and may not know enough yet to decide whether permitted development rights apply or whether a full planning permission is required for what you intend to build. Engaging with a builder or enlightening any adjoining owners, therefore, comes much further on in the process, and I will explain later the correct time for this action to take place (See Book Three: 'Attributes and Constraints').

Permitted Development Option

At this point, it is worth highlighting that for some domestic and commercial residential projects there is an opportunity to avail of permitted development rights, often referred to PD. Permitted development rights exist as part of the Planning Act 2008 whereby given the small size and nature of the intended work, obtaining a planning permission is not obligatory.

There are naturally some unique circumstances where the planning rules might have to allow an inappropriate extension or development without any planning scrutiny, as with some PD projects, for instance (see Book Two: 'Planning and Permitted Development'). There are some atrocious examples of extensions and structures erected throughout the country, often under the direction of a builder providing a so-called 'free design service' which really is nothing more than a means to convince their customers an all-inclusive price is an excellent value. I should add there is nothing 'free' when it comes to construction, and finalising tender price correctly is more than a casual arrangement with a builder. In Book Four I discuss the pitfalls associated with this type of approach where homeowners and laypeople especially, without the expertise of a qualified architect, behind them are more often than not left exposed in relation to construction costs. They can also some-

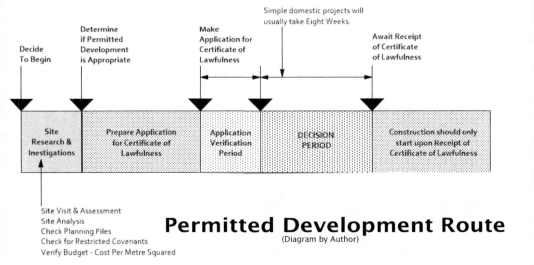

Permitted Development Route
(Diagram by Author)

A typical example of a permitted development roof conversion solution in isolation of all other surrounding properties.
An exercise in building more than a display of architectural design for the Property. (Image by Author)

times be at serious risk in terms of adherence to planning requirements, even with employing permitted development rights.

There are always going to be pitfalls, and homeowners especially should be alert when they are told they do not need planning permission when what they intend falls under permitted development. That may be true, but homeowners should ensure they secure a Certificate of Lawfulness prior to any construction commencing.

Nine times out of ten where the architect's design expertise is absent, new builds of this calibre are always out of architectural context, usually out of scale/proportion with what already exists, and offer no enhancement or recognition to what already exists (see Chapter 5: 'Built Environment, Context, and Character').

The majority of these projecting roofs (often referred to as a 'dormer roof' or 'dormer window') are usually devoid of any sensible relationship to the existing character of the existing building itself. They also tend to decimate the character of the original building, the adjoining build-

With this parade of terraced roof conversions; individual preferences are managed by incorporating the party wall structure between each property. (Image by Author)

ings, and often the street or road generally. Just because they are located at the rear of the property under what permitted development rights allow does not lessen the visual discord they create, as they are often very visible due to their location and orientation to public view, and they will forever remain a lump on the roofscape. The planning authority is totally powerless in many cases to prevent such eye-gouging experiences, but this type of development is left to those less interested in the manner in which their property should evolve on an architectural level.

Not all roof conversions, however, are lacking in architectural design and recognition of what already exists. It does not take much to be aware of what is actually happening architecturally and usually there is a very simple, cost-effective solution.

Take a Sanity Check

Take some time and think about your new building or extension as a physical entity, an element that has visual presence and with a functional use. Always remember, buildings will occupy a footprint on the ground and will occupy space in the air as a three-dimensional volumetric entity. Your objective is to demonstrate that your design proposal provides a 'good fit', has relevance, references what is already there, and is something that you can be proud of, naturally.

Adopting this mindset is an excellent beginning and applies whether you opt to employ permitted development rights or choose to make a submission for a planning permission.

When you begin giving some thought to the form and size of space or spaces you want and consider with your architect and how your new extension or building

In this example homeowners and their designers were clearly alert to the value of the existing architectural features above the first floor windows and succeeded in retaining the architectural character of this parade of terrace properties with these more sympathetic roof conversions.
These are roof conversions to the rear of the properties but clearly visible from the public highway.
(Image by Author)

might best fit in with your existing property and the surrounding properties, you start to think about some of the practicalities associated with your personal preferences and evaluate these against what design options might be possible and what is sensible, visually attractive, practical to build, and financially affordable as a combined enterprise.

There is always room for exciting, innovative architectural design solutions, but this usually results when the whole of the pre-planning process, and the architectural design process in particular, is delegated to the expertise of a trained architect.

There are occasions where not too much innovation is called for given the nature of the place or the nature of an existing building you could be dealing with. In the final analysis, it might be deemed more sensible, pragmatic, and even appropriate to employ a design solution which reflects the existing form and character of the existing building itself or that of the surrounding character. That, too, is equally valid, as not every project needs to follow or should follow the 'grand design' mantra. Sometimes that is for the birds and out of kilter with the reality of what your project might entail on a number of levels, and for many that might include the available budget.

Keep in the back of your mind, then, what is more likely to be an appropriate design solution for your property. As a self-manager/client or agent, question what might be more real for your client - more doable, as it were, and reasonable in terms of satisfying your local planning authority, as not all planning authorities are the same or have the same emphasis or requirements. Your focus in this regard is to acquaint yourself with what is prescribed for your site or property's location with the local authority's neighbourhood plan or local plan. This comes first and foremost, even before you start dreaming about your new building.

Equally important is the question of what can be afforded. I would ask you to give this matter some serious consideration before you instruct any work to commence, because there are too many instances where projects have to stop due to insufficient funds to complete the project on-site (see Book Two: 'Making Your Project Work Financially'). In Book Two, I explain what strategy I employ when discussing matters related to financing my client's projects.

In my experience, some clients have a wish list of many things which, when examined and analysed in relation to the essence of the project and their primary objective, are neither necessary nor practical and sometimes not affordable. As a self-manager /client, stay grounded in your thinking and try to manage your expectations and your budget in a realistic way. This also applies where you are managing the project business on behalf of your client, as you have a greater responsibility to ensure your client is made aware of what is happening as matters progress and especially which direction the budget is heading.

I discuss a number of aspects surrounding project costs in more detail in Book Four of this series wherein I highlight the local planning authority's fee charges you should expect when making a planning

Engaging with a qualified architect from the beginning will always ensure a better investment for your project. (Image by ergonofis)

submission. You will also have the benefit of what professional fees you should expect to pay and what professional service you should expect. I also focus on actual building costs in order to provide you with a good steer on what you should reasonably expect, which again will provide you with a good overview for you to assess whether your project is affordable and whether you need to make some adjustments in order to achieve much of what you would like but maybe not everything.

Therefore, as a self-manager, before you even spend money on testing a planning submission, these books will give you a valuable heads-up and lend you some direction on what may or may not be affordable and sensible for you. For the agent acting for their clients, it will provide you with a very useful guide in how to present project information for your clients' consideration and instruction.

Chapter Nine

Collecting Your Thoughts

Managing Expectations

I am aware that when it comes to making a planning submission most people, especially homeowners, think of drawings and only drawings. Indeed, there are a number of options when it comes employing your agent. Having a set of planning drawings prepared for you can range from a draughtsperson to a surveyor, an engineer, or the local technical drawing teacher, all of whom may be competent in preparing drawings and some may even be skilled in preparing planning drawings. For the most part, this is always considered to be the 'cheapest' option, and what you pay for is certainly what you get.

The draughtsperson or person who may be capable of producing technical drawings will not necessarily provide any meaningful site analysis or collaborate with you in-depth in relation to assessing your brief or what architectural design solution might be appropriate for your site or for your specific user purposes. They tend not to question or investigate the site for what it is and represents and do not assess and analyse any attributes and constraints where they exist. In fact, they are not equipped to provide you with much in-depth professional expertise and guidance because they are not trained to that level. Generally,

they provide you with a set of planning drawings for a fee based on what you ask for and it ends there; then, you get what you pay for.

However, I would like to believe that where such agents refer to this pre-planning book series, they are keen to assist their clients in a more meaningful and robust way. For instance, being more alert to architectural design principles and having more awareness of architectural context and character, site, and project analysis combined with asking pertinent questions in relation to the overall design solution will produce a design solution where the construction process has been considered in parallel with the pre-planning design considerations. It goes far beyond just a basic set of line drawings.

Book Four, *Making The Planning Submission,* explores this topic in much more detail, but for now I merely wish to bring these particular matters to your attention. I am alert to the fact that many homeowner clients believe that once the planning drawings are complete and planning permission is obtained, their builder can start construction the next day. This is certainly not the case and if a builder says he can, then you most certainly have the wrong builder, if indeed 'builder' is the correct terminology.

Because I have been called in by clients to identify and sort delivery problems on site, I am aware also that unless a level of thinking has been employed in the concept design process from the beginning, the planning drawings are usually only satisfactory for obtaining a planning decision. By this I mean that the planning drawings were prepared in total isolation from building construction considerations, which can leave the client exposed to the demands of the builder and some very expensive rectification work. Indeed, the non-architect agents in many cases tend not to even concern themselves with building control and thus it is often overlooked by design.

A Word for the Architect

I need to highlight once more the real added value of appointing a person who will bring professional expertise on a number of levels from the start and see your project through from beginning to end. I know some property owners will be told (usually by builders) they can save themselves a ton of architect's fees by eliminating any professional involvement, especially after the planning stage.

Truly, this is a false economy, even more so in relation to project management beyond the pre-planning stage. Managing the many on-site processes with your building contractor at the helm will always leave you (the employer, as defined within the building contract) exposed. I have witnessed too many situations of this nature,

(Image by Fred Moon)

and in all cases the client has regretted not engaging a responsible professional from the beginning. Naturally, I am biased, and I make no apologies for knowing better.

How do I know that? Well, it is because I can refer to the numerous occasions in my career where this has been the situation. I have often been appointed to sort out the chaos generated by others for the client, sometimes even demonstrating to the client that making a fresh planning submission would be a better option. In other words, they need to start again, and they usually agree if they decide not to abandon the project or move property altogether.

In other cases, a dispute between the contractor and the employer under the contract (assuming there is a contract in place, which there should be) has left the project at a standstill and appointing another contractor was the only sensible option remaining for my client. Dealing with builders and contractors can be a complex business; even qualified architects need to keep their wits about them. Some are smart operators with plenty of operating knowhow behind them. Keep in mind that experienced clients know the value of working with a qualified architect. They would never expose themselves to the vulnerabilities connected with a building project. All projects are simple until something goes wrong, then chaos ensues.

They recognise the seven years spent studying and training with some additional years in practice would indicate the level of expertise and commitment qualified architects offer as a starting

(Image by Linkedin Sales Solutions)

point and are bound by the code of practice of the Architects Registration Board (ARB).

Qualified architects are best placed to manage both the planning submission process and the construction process that follows and can do it all as one joint exercise. They recognise issues like attributes and constraints as a natural part of their site analysis and much more besides, just like a lawyer or a surgeon understands the complexities and wide-ranging events that can occur within their respective professions.

If you are not totally sure of any aspect, your architect will assist you in deciphering which options are worth exploring further and suggest what would be appropriate for your project situation, just as surgeons would with their patients or lawyers do for their clients.

Qualified architects are trained to take on board all the issues involved in making appropriate design decisions relating to planning submission but also evaluate this against creating a sensible detail design solution when it comes to the actual building process further down the line at the site.

(Image from WikiMedia)

Thinking Ahead

Contemplating a new building, extension, or roof conversion means thinking ahead. It means identifying what might happen and having a strategy for designing out and problematic issues. It means getting the balance right when weighing various options and alternative solutions and being able to make decisions with a measure of confidence. It is always far more economical to have problematic issues identified and designed out from the very beginning, prior to making your planning submission, as they tend to reappear during the construction stage on-site if they are not addressed correctly.

Clearly there is heaps more to know about the pre-planning process, but having a headsup on what you might expect is a good start. The intention of this Book One of the pre-planning series is to introduce you to what you need to be aware of and what you might expect when it comes to first thinking about having your property built or extended and then having a planning submission prepared to obtain your planning permission.

I know from experience that when you are contemplating a project you need to know more than just somebody telling you that you will need an architect. Obviously, an architect is a better option. By taking on board the insights and in-

formation provided by this book, I am sure much of the process surrounding pre-planning will now be more meaningful for you. Now that you have a good grasp of what is involved and what is expected when preparing a planning submission,

Having a strategy for obtaining your planning permission is always a worthwhile investment of time.   (Image by Vlada Karpovich)

you now need to know more about how to actually execute the work either as a self-manager/client or as an agent. Consequently, the subject matter and insights set out in Books Two, Three, and Four are even more revealing. Armed with this information, you will also find that making decisions for your project can be made with a greater degree of confidence.

Chapter Ten

Where to Go From Here

Important Information Resource

In this book, I wanted to introduce you to the rudiments surrounding the business of obtaining a planning permission. That is, of course, if a planning permission is an appropriate option for you, because adopting the permitted development route might be a possible solution for what you are considering (see Book Two: 'Planning and Permitted Development').

This book is really a precursor to the whole planning procurement process. I want you to have relevant information which will allow you to make some fundamental decisions about how you might proceed from here. Essentially, I want you have a reasonably good overview of what is involved when it comes to thinking about your project and then be able to assess your options to achieve your planning permission objective. Being armed with a general overview of the planning process together with a grasp of some of the specifics associated with planning, you will find yourself in a good place to decide where you would like to go from here with your project.

As a first-time self-manager/client having completed *How to Get Started*, you now have sufficient information to decide whether self-managing your own project and the pre-planning process in particular might be what you would like to do. You might also decide it is not a wise or prudent investment of your time and find that you really do not to wish to undertake a new specialism with all that it entails. You might decide, therefore, looking at things in the round that appointing a qualified professional is an appropriate option for you. Whatever you decide at this point is a good decision, having reviewed what is required in making a planning submission.

Should you decide that progressing through the pre-planning process is manageable but you would benefit from some further step-by-step insights surrounding the actual actions that need to be taken or to sharpen up your current knowledge and skills, that is a good decision too.

I would suggest you now need to equip yourself with a more detailed account of the topics referred to here in *How to Get Started* in order to move on to the next level so you can function with a greater effect or represent your client in a more robust fashion. You will need a strategy and an information resource that will help you through the various steps necessary for preparing your planning submission.

Book Two, *Research and Investigations*, is the next book in the pre-planning series and does exactly that. It is the natural book to follow on with your planning journey. It takes you through what has to be done when it comes to your research and investigation work and much more. The topics discussed provide a more in-depth account of what has to be undertaken and it includes a simple methodology for managing your pre-planning process.

You will see from these topics that there is a great deal of in-depth information examined, and much of it will set you thinking about some of the potential pitfalls and tricky bits to watch out for as well as a step-by-step approach for undertaking your research and investigations for your project.

PLANNING PERMISSION EXPERTISE FOR BUILDINGS AND EXTENSIONS

A Step-by-Step Guide by a Chartered Architect

Dr. WILLIAM J. HOGAN-O'NEILL RIBA. ARB.

Book Two - Research and Investigations
Pre-Planning Series

Architect®
Knowhow.

Book Two - The Green Book
Research and Investigations

Know What You Are Dealing With

Reason for Research and Investigation Previous Planning Applications

Adapting a Planning Permission

Previous Planning Refusals

Reasons for Refusal

Lapsed Planning Permission

Changing an Existing Planning Permission

Planning Conditions and What They Mean

Your Initial Thoughts

What Do You Know

The Site and the Property Owner

The Research Process

How to Search the Planning Files

What the Delegated Report Says/Means

Assessing Your Situation

Why a Briefing Document

Site Survey, Site Analysis, and Concept Development

Gathering Intelligence for Your Planning Submission

Keep Your Project Private

Property for Life or to Sell On

Creating Added Value Property Valuation

Making Your Project Work Financially

Book Three - The Brown Book

Attributes and Constraints

- This book provides a real in-depth account on issues that can have a profound impact on your project.

- It deals with a heap of issues and potential risks where some might be presented to you as a result of your research and investigations. Matters such as restrictive covenants, party wall matters or flood risk for example, all of which have potential cost implications and sometimes even prohibitive costs, which, can potentially put the brakes on your project.

- Constraints therefore, will influence the pre-planning preparation process where ultimately the architectural design solution will necessitate some serious decision-making for your planning submission purposes. Constraints will also, highlight potential implications when dealing with matters relating to the construction process which for you is the ultimate goal.

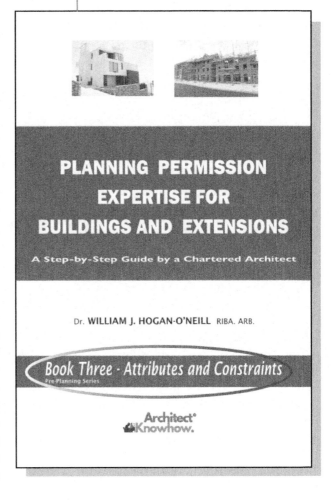

PLANNING PERMISSION EXPERTISE FOR BUILDINGS AND EXTENSIONS

A Step-by-Step Guide by a Chartered Architect

Dr. **WILLIAM J. HOGAN-O'NEILL** RIBA. ARB.

Book Three - Attributes and Constraints
Pre-Planning Series

Architect®
Knowhow.

Book Four - The Blue Book

The Planning Submission

- Walks you through the process of identifying what information and planning documents to assemble for your planning submission.

- Sets out the likely costs and fees associated with obtaining a planning permission and where additional costs might arise depending on the nature of your site location and project specifics.

- Provides an in-depth account as to why the pre-application process is a valuable option to avail of.

- Explains how to prepare for your pre-application meeting with your local planning authority.

- Details the options available to you resulting from the pre-application meeting and acting on the local planning authority's pre-application written advice.

- Discusses the process to finalise and correct your design proposal before you make your final planning submission.

- Explains why aspects of building control should be considered in parallel when preparing your planning submission so as to make the overall project sensible and cost-effective.

- Illuminates the differences between a full plans approval and a building notices together with costs associated with making an application for approval and the best time within the overall process to make your application.

- Establishes the role of the architect and what you might reasonably expect their services to include.

- Outlines aspects relating to the tender process and why you should approach this very important element of the work with a measure of care to avoid being manipulated by unscrupulous operators.

- Offers insight into what specialist consultants may be valuable for your individual project, such as a structural engineer or a hydrologist.

- All of this and more is discussed in Book Four.

PLANNING PERMISSION
EXPERTISE FOR
BUILDINGS AND EXTENSIONS

A Step-by-Step Guide by a Chartered Architect

Dr. **WILLIAM J. HOGAN-O'NEILL** RIBA. ARB.

Book Four - Making The Planning Submission
Pre-Planning

Architect®
Knowhow.

A Big Thank You

Thank you so much for investing in this book. My aspiration for you is that you have extracted a great deal of value from it and prepared you for what you should expect when embarking on a building project. I am hoping too, you have gained better insight into what needs to be considered right at the very beginning. That is the primary purpose of this first book in the series.

If you are a homeowner/self-manager/client, you have hopefully fulfilled your objective in gaining a better overview of the process involved and some greater clarity about deciding whether managing your project yourself is the correct option for you or if engaging a consultant might be a more convenient option from the beginning. Appointing an architect should never be considered as an extra cost, as I know some would like you to believe. Instead, consider the architect's fee as a natural part of the overall project costs, just as foundations are a natural and necessary project cost. An architect is a registered professional consultant, and like any other professionally qualified consultant such as a surgeon or lawyer, for instance, professional fees are paid for their professional service and expertise.

Equally, if you are a new property owner about to embark on a development project, I expect you have grasped the concept that, with matters relating to planning, there is a process to follow. Having a clearer understanding of what that process is, what some of the tricky bits and situations might mean for your project, and how you might set about managing the various events is a crucial part of ensuring your project will return a sensible profit.

For the agent/consultant already providing planning services or a student about to embark on an architectural, engineering, project management, or construction career, it is my intention to leave you with a deeper insight about how to better navigate the pre-planning process for your client. I would like to believe you now have a better appreciation of what questions to ask of yourself in order to provide a professional service to your clients. Adopting and applying options highlighted here is a worthwhile route to explore for your projects and will encourage you to examine your practice in much greater detail. But, your education does not stop with this book alone.

Everything I have highlighted for you here is based on my own experiences and practical knowledge I have acquired during my time in professional practice. If there is one certainty to encourage you to remain mindful of at all times, it is this: that you take control and remain in control of events when leading the pre-planning process on your own behalf or that of your clients.

Best of luck with your project!

William

The Perfect Checklist for Getting Organised and Keeping Control of Your Project!

www.architectknowhow.com

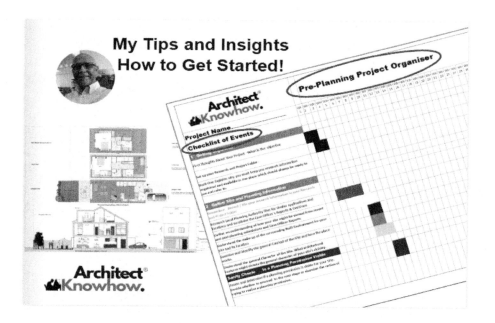

Get Yourself Organised with these 10 Actions:

Getting Organised

Gather Site and Planning Information

Verify Status of the Site / Property

Examine Your Planning Options

Carry Out Detail Checks

Commence Concept Design Development

Prepare for Your Pre-Application

Prepare Your Planning Drawings & Documents

Decision to proceed with Planning Submission

Planning Period Begins

Bibliography:

Merriam, D. (2004). The complete Guide to Zoning: How to Navigate the Comp expensive Maze, Planning, environmental, and Land- Use Law (1st ed.). McGr Education.

Royal Institute of Town Planning. (2020, September). Planning Through Zoning
/rtpi.org.uk/research/2020/september/planning-through-zoning/
(Accessed:25/05/21).

Panda, I (2020, October27). Context and Building in Architecture. Reviewed http://ivypanda.com/essays/context-and-building-in-architecture/
(Accessed August 2021)

Gaine, M. (2021) How to Get Planning Permission: An insider's Secrets. S Books. London.

Hogan-O'Neill, W. (2021) Prefabricated and Modular Architecture (1st e Vergne:crowood.

Local Government Planning. (n.d.). Https://Www.Localgov.Co.Uk/ Planning. Retrieved 17 October 2021, from https:// www.localgov.co.uk/Planning.

Skopeliti, C. (2021, September 11). Minister 'to ditch overhaul of planning laws' after critism. Https://Www.Theguardian.Com/Politics/ 2021/Sep/11/Ministers-to-Ditch-Overhaul-of-Planning-Laws-after-Criticism.
Retrieved 12 September 2021, from https://www.theguardian.com/ politics/2021/sep/11/ministers-to-ditch-overhaul-of-planning-laws-after-criticism

William has been in architectural practice for over thirty seven years and during this time he has designed and completed many buildings employing Prefabricated and Modular Technology. He is recognised as a subject expert in this design specialism and was invited to write this book on the subject by a UK publisher.

If you are a student, a design practitioner or a developer, this is an importance reference for gaining a valuable insight of this fast growing alternative for building design and procurement.

Available on Amazon

Opinion ☰ Book review

Review

Angus McFarlane recommends this book to structural engineers who wish to advance their knowledge of prefabrication and modular construction.

Prefabricated and modular architecture: Aligning design with manufacture and assembly

Author: William J. Hogan-O'Neill
Publisher: The Crowood Press Ltd
Price: £20.00
ISBN: 978-1-78500-806-1

THIS BOOK IS A MUST-READ FOR ARCHITECTS, ENGINEERS AND OTHER CONSTRUCTION PROFESSIONALS that wish to further their knowledge about design for manufacture and assembly (DfMA) in relation to prefabrication and offsite manufacture (OSM).

The book covers the whole gamut of prefabrication ranging from its early mixture, through the negative perception of post-war prefabricated housing 'prehaps' and system-built tower blocks, to the renewed interest in OSM today.

The main theme of the book is that architects should embrace DfMA methodology as an integral part of their design process so that they can maintain a significant contribution to the construction industry in the future. The author contends that as architects gain experience in the design of different prefabricated buildings, they will transform current practice and promote prefabricated architecture so that it eventually becomes recognised as a new discipline in its own right.

The author calls this new discipline PAMA (prefabricated and modular architecture) and, for PAMA to become relevant, it will require significant input from trained architects who are prepared to adopt standardisation and manufacturing as an intrinsic element of their design process.

It is emphasised that prefabricated architecture is not constrained. It relies on a small number of simple concepts involving manufacturing processes that already exist, namely parts, components and sub-assemblies, panelised systems, hybrid construction – comprising conventional construction plus panelising; and fully modularised systems – consisting of 3D volumetric modules.

The book clearly defines the difference between panelised and modularisation, which are terms that are often used interchangeably. Panelisation consists of 2D elements (columns, floors and walls) and is essentially an enhancement to the conventional construction process. Whereas modularisation consists of 3D volumetric modules.

This book highlights that volumetric modules can consist of complete buildings or parts of a building. The modules are usually completely fitted out with fixtures and fittings, leaving only the final connections to be completed as part of the on-site assembly process. Sometimes referred to as 'plug-and-play', it is also noted that volumetric modular building is the only medium that can enable 95% completion of the buildings superstructure form within a factory environment, with the remaining 5% being the final assembly process on site.

It is emphasised that modular buildings result in significant time savings on site because they are

created in a fully constructed using a factory-based manufacturing process, with less time required for their on-site assembly. Also highlighted is that modular buildings can lead to significant savings in substructure and foundation work because they tend to be much lighter than the conventional equivalent. However, to gain the maximum benefits for the project, the decision to go modular must be made early in the concept design stage.

The book states that the greatest aesthetic impact is achieved in prefabrication when the connection forming part of the structure are expressed as part of the architecture of the building, i.e. the building's structural engineering enhances the architectural design. Consequently, the structural engineering becomes part of the architecture. Additionally, it is emphasised that the building services engineering can also contribute in a similar manner and examples of the Lloyds building in London and the Pompidou Centre in Paris are presented.

Additionally, regarding aesthetics, it is stated that the current housing sector (and some other sectors, such as schools) are fast followers of a standardised approach and that there is a demand for each building or project to express its own individuality, which, in former years, would have been difficult to achieve with prefabricated and modular designs. Consequently, the book notes that customisation can be included in the concept design by using individuality to the elements and modules of a project. Indeed although not mentioned in the book, some Japanese manufacturers of modular buildings have introduced mass-customisation methodology.

From a sustainability perspective, the book highlights that factory-produced buildings have less waste usage, less pollution, less wastage, and less environmental impact when compared with conventional construction.

The final portion of the book deals with the issues in transporting prefabricated elements from the factory to the site and it highlights the need for planning regarding element dimensions, weight, and preparing the delivery route to site.

I have no hesitation in recommending this book to those construction professionals that wish to advance their knowledge of prefabrication and modular construction. The only criticism is that book intimates that DfMA is part of PAMA, whereas the converse would unlikely be more correct.

Angus McFarlane
Angus McFarlane is the Structural Engineering Lead in Laing O'Rourke's Engineering Excellence Group in Sydney, Australia. He is a passionate practitioner of modular construction utilising DfMA.

August 2021 | theStructuralEngineer.org

Printed in Great Britain
by Amazon

86390813R00081